T0101968

100

THINGS PRODUCTIVE PEOPLE DO

LITTLE LESSONS IN GETTING THINGS DONE

NIGEL CUMBERLAND

First published by Nicholas Brealey Publishing in 2022

An imprint of John Murray Press
A division of Hodder & Stoughton Ltd,
An Hachette UK company

1

Copyright © Nigel Cumberland 2022

The right of Nigel Cumberland to be identified as the Author of the Work has been asserted by him in accordance with the Copyright, Designs and Patents Act 1988.

All rights reserved. No part of this publication may be reproduced, stored in a retrieval system, or transmitted, in any form or by any means without the prior written permission of the publisher, nor be otherwise circulated in any form of binding or cover other than that in which it is published and without a similar condition being imposed on the subsequent purchaser.

A CIP catalogue record for this title is available from the British Library

Hardback ISBN 978 1 529 38997 5
eBook ISBN 978 1 529 38999 9

Typeset by KnowledgeWorks Global Ltd.

Printed and bound in Great Britain by Clays Ltd, Elcograf S.p.A.

John Murray Press policy is to use papers that are natural, renewable and recyclable products and made from wood grown in sustainable forests. The logging and manufacturing processes are expected to conform to the environmental regulations of the country of origin.

John Murray Press
Carmelite House
50 Victoria Embankment
London EC4Y 0DZ

Nicholas Brealey Publishing
Hachette Book Group
Market Place, Center 53, State Street
Boston, MA 02109, USA

www.nicholasbrealey.com

This book is dedicated to my son, Zeb, my stepdaughter, Yasmine, and to all those wishing to be highly productive and successful in all aspects of their lives and careers.

'The best kind of hackers are those who spend their time learning, implementing and benefiting from every productivity tool they can find.'

Contents

About the author

Nigel Cumberland is the co-founder of The Silk Road Partnership, a leading global provider of executive coaching and leadership training solutions to some of the world's leading organizations. He has lived and worked in locations as diverse as Hong Kong, Glasgow, Budapest, Santiago, Dubai, Singapore, Guatemala City, Kuala Lumpur, London and Shanghai, gaining experiences and wisdom that have helped teach him what it takes to succeed and be highly productive in all aspects of his life and work.

Previously, Nigel worked as a multinational finance director with Coats plc, as well as for some of the world's leading recruitment firms including Adecco. He is a Fellow of the UK's Chartered Institute of Management Accountants. He co-created an award-winning recruitment firm based in Hong Kong and China, which he later sold to Hays plc. Educated at Cambridge University, UK, Nigel is an extensively qualified executive coach and leadership training professional. In 2016, he was made a Freeman of the City of London.

He is the author of a large number of self-help and leadership books, among the most recent of which are: *100 Things Successful Leaders Do: Little Lessons in Leadership* (Nicholas Brealey Publishing, 2020), *100 Things Millionaires Do: Little Lessons in Creating Wealth* (Nicholas Brealey Publishing, 2019), *The Ultimate Management Book* (John Murray Learning, 2018), *100 Things Successful People Do: Little Exercises for Successful Living* (John Murray Learning, 2016), *Secrets of Success at Work: 50 Techniques to Excel* (Hodder & Stoughton, 2014), *Finding and Hiring Talent in a Week* (John Murray Learning, 2016) and *Leading Teams in a Week* (John Murray Learning, 2016).

Nigel is married to a wonderful woman named Evelyn, who spends her time as an artist. He has two inspiring children – a son, Zeb, and a stepdaughter, Yasmine.

Introduction

Being really productive never happens by accident. It's always a conscious and well-planned choice.

Are you ready to super-charge your life and career? You've picked up the perfect book to serve as your guide – to help you master the key habits, skills and behaviours to enable you to be productive in all aspects of your daily life and work. It's fantastic that you are reading this book – that you want to become more productive in various aspects of your life. The world is awaiting you to turn into the most productive person you are capable of, whether you are:

- starting in a new job and find yourself overwhelmed
- leading a team for the first time and want them to exceed expectations
- wishing to succeed in managing your time, focus and energy in your high school or university studies
- managing your household budget and chores
- helping run a voluntary organization at weekends.

When you think of being productive, who comes to mind? Hard-working entrepreneurs like Elon Musk and Jeff Bezos perhaps? Friends who only work three days a week and seem to achieve so much? Your son who successfully studied for an online university degree while holding down two jobs? Or your boss who is so efficient and always leaves the office by 6pm at the latest each day and never works at weekends?

I've coached hundreds of people in organizations as diverse as the United Nations, the World Bank Group, global banks and multinationals, local tech start-ups, governments, schools and NGOs. All these individuals wanted to work on aspects of their personal productivity. I've heard about every productivity challenge and success story you can imagine, and as a result this book should be able to help you no matter how you need or wish to become more productive.

The main lesson I have picked up is a simple one – too many people fail to work on all aspects of their productivity toolbox, leaving them with underutilized skills and strengths, and hanging onto weaknesses and bad habits. This results in them being much less productive than they want to be.

Not you ... working through this book is your opportunity to sit down and think about yourself, giving you time to ask yourself how you want to work smarter in order to use your time and energy more productively – and exceed any goals and objectives you need to achieve.

Treat this book as your trusted companion. Through 100 short chapters, you'll learn to make sense of the pieces you need to slot together to create a productive life. You'll explore what being productive means to you through topics including:

- good time management
- prioritizing well
- planning optimally
- effective meetings
- learning, replicating and practising
- optimal emails and communications
- working well with others
- using ideal tools and apps
- strengthening habits and behaviours.

How to use this book

Every chapter in this book features a new idea that will help you get closer to your goals. In each chapter, the ideas are introduced and explained on the first page and the second page features exercises and activities, some small and some large, for you to start doing today.

Don't overlook the activities. The tasks you've been set have been specifically designed to give you the optimal mindset, habits, skills, relationships and behaviours needed to maximize your chances of leadership success. Some of them will surprise you, some will challenge you, others will seem simple and obvious. All of them are important in building the portfolio of skills you need for becoming more productive. Completing them will set you on the path to developing a productivity mindset and gaining expertise in working smart. These things aren't easy to achieve and few people are willing to invest the required time and effort. Highly productive people do.

You'll find many activities to do straight away and some for later, depending on your current situation and challenges as well as your many plans and goals. If an idea or suggestion doesn't seem helpful now, put it to one side and return to it later.

Who am I to talk about being productive?

This book draws on the wisdom I've gained from coaching and mentoring leaders from all over the world for the past 20 years. From global CEOs to struggling entrepreneurs, through to leaders in the public sector and charities to first-time managers just starting out on their leadership careers. All of them have something to share about the journey of becoming highly productive.

Their experiences combine with my own wisdom gained through some incredibly personal highs and lows. From profound lessons I've learned through:

- pushing myself to become a regional financial director with a FTSE100 company at the age of only 26
- heading subsidiaries, in various countries, of a range of multinational companies
- creating and taking the lead of a charity foundation
- being on the leadership teams of various tech start-ups including in the educational robotics and internet spaces
- sitting on the board of directors of entities including international schools.

Most importantly, I have learned how to value and enjoy being a leader, and to appreciate how I am able to positively impact the lives and careers of so many people and communities.

From all my work and experience, I have drawn up the most essential 100 things you need for getting things done as smartly and efficiently as possible. I hope all the advice in this book helps you achieve all of your dreams, goals and tasks – to create the success story you truly deserve.

UNDERSTAND YOUR NEED TO BE PRODUCTIVE

Visualize what you want – then go and get it.

Let's start at the beginning. *Why* do you want to be more productive? This is a question I ask those I am coaching, after they've shared a desire to be more productive than they are now.

There are so many possible reasons:

- I want to be the first to finish any task.
- I want to have more free time for other things.
- I want to be less drained at the end of the day.
- I want to make my work easier to complete.
- I want to sleep well without worrying about work.
- I want to involve others by sharing my workload.
- I want to overcome the stress of a large to-do list.
- I want to show my boss I'm capable.
- I want to leave work on time for once.
- I want to exceed expectations.

Each of us is unique and guided by our personality, work environment, past experiences and role models. A priority for you might be something to 'avoid at all costs' for someone else: you might want to multi-task effortlessly, while someone else just wants to focus on one task at a time; you might want to rush through your to-do list, spending as little time as possible on every task, whereas someone else might want to complete every task to perfection.

Discovering *why* you want to be more productive will help you know *how* – how you can become more productive in ways that will optimally help you achieve your goals.

Chapter 1

Discover what being productive means to you

Ask yourself why you are not fully productive right now and what has drawn you to this book. What are you looking to fix? These suggestions might help you think through your own reasons:

- Do you feel you could be faster and more efficient?
- Has your line manager complained about the quality of your work?
- Are you continually stressed and overwhelmed by your workload?
- Are you tired of spending hours completing manual tasks?
- Do you already have a high level of productivity and just want to learn some new techniques?

First, make a list of the challenges you want to overcome. Now turn them into positive-sounding, productivity-focused outcomes that you'll be motivated to achieve. This is a visualization exercise in 'starting with the end in mind' and in recognizing that we all respond better to positive goals and outcomes than we do to negative ones. If the above five examples of challenges were yours, then your corresponding outcomes might be written as:

- I work in a very fast, efficient and productive way with everything I need to complete.
- My line manager is continually impressed with my high-quality work.
- I comfortably manage my workload free of any stress or sense of overwhelm.
- I successfully find ways of efficiently and smartly completing tasks that used to be slow and manual.
- My work performance and levels of productivity are consistently rising.

Find the appropriate tools and solutions

Once you've visualized what you want to achieve, you're well placed to work through this book and ready to decide which of the 100 things are key for you to implement today.

KNOW WHAT NEEDS TO BE DONE

If you don't have a plan, how will you know where to start?

In a world of so much uncertainty, simply knowing and writing down what you need to do can be very calming and reassuring. But having a to-do list is more than a 'nice to have' reminder of the tasks awaiting you, it can actually help drive your performance by making things clearer for you. This was the conclusion of 2011 research from Florida State University which found that when we list our unfinished tasks, we substantially reduce the mental distraction from having things to complete, leaving us free to successfully do the work at hand.

Given this benefit of having a to-do list, even one written on the back of a napkin is much better than not having one at all. But highly productive people take their 'to-do listing' to another level. They know that only by creating and keeping an updated written and structured to-do list can they be sure of optimizing their productivity. This is supported by 2016 research by Shamarukh Chowdhury at Canada's Carleton University who surveyed 300 undergraduates about how they create and maintain their to-do lists and how their choices impact their productivity and success in completing their tasks in a timely manner. He concluded that:

- those who created more formal to-do lists procrastinated less compared with those who only had random lists of pending tasks
- those who regularly updated and referred to their to-do lists were more conscientiousness than other students.

It's time for you to become a to-do list expert!

Create a to-do list ...

Where and how you make a list is your choice – it can be in a paper journal or notebook, recorded online in a Word or Excel document or stored in a productivity app on your smartphone. If you're not sure what works best for you, try experimenting by:

- maintaining a list of your pending tasks in a paper notebook and writing a new list each week on a new page
- creating an Excel spreadsheet which you can easily keep updated and print out if needed
- using one of the many online planning and scheduling tools (which are explored in later chapters).

You'll quickly find out what method you prefer. I've tried many and today I maintain a hand-written to-do list, so that I can feel the satisfaction of being able to cross out tasks as I complete them.

... and stick to it

The key is to be consistent and to keep your to-do list updated on a daily or weekly basis. Do this by referring to your list every day, ensuring that you tick off what you have completed and updating your list as new tasks arise or the details of existing tasks change.

WORK IN SHORT BURSTS

Work with your attention span – not against it.

Although there's no definitive answer to the question of how long a human's concentration span is, studies over recent years have concluded that we lose concentration in a matter of minutes. A UK study in 2017 conducted by Skipton Building Society discovered that the average attention span is only 14 minutes, depending on what you are doing and with whom. Their research showed the average length of concentration in different settings:

Activity	Average length of concentration
In a meeting	13 minutes
Talking to someone with a boring voice	6 minutes
Having a work phone call	7 minutes
Reading a book	15 minutes
Social situation with a friend	29 minutes

So, the next time your mind drifts in a staff meeting, or you start daydreaming while drafting a report, don't feel guilty. We are not wired to be able to focus on one thing for very long, and in our world of social media, internet and information overload, this is only likely to get worse.

Productive people understand this and are careful to work on tasks only for a few minutes before taking a break. One way of emulating them is to follow the Pomodoro technique which was created by Francesco Cirillo in the 1980s. This is a time management technique that forces you to work in short bursts interspersed with breaks, with the aim of aligning periods of focused work with your attention span.

Let's put it into action.

Chapter 3

Practise the Pomodoro technique

Cirillo's original model suggests you follow this pattern of working:

1 Choose the work you want to focus on.
2 Work on that task for 25 minutes, using an alarm to let you know when the 25 minutes are over.
3 Stop what you're doing and take a 5–10-minute break.
4 Work for another 25 minutes, followed by another short break.
5 After completing three rounds of 25 minutes, take a longer break for 20–30 minutes.

Repeat this pattern all day if needed.

Have a go, and tweak the numbers if you need to so that it works better for you (for example, increase the 25 minutes to half an hour). The key is to systematically work in timed short bursts and then to take short breaks to allow your concentration to recover ready for another round of work.

STAY HEALTHY TO STAY PRODUCTIVE

Eat well, sleep enough and move more – for optimum productivity.

You can implement all the latest and coolest productivity hacks, but if you don't look after yourself physically, you'll fail. Adrenalin and a few cups of coffee might keep you productive today, but eventually you will crash.

There are three areas of your physical health that impact your ability to work well – sleep, exercise and nutrition.

- Not having enough sleep takes its toll on your ability to focus, concentrate, think and communicate. One piece of US research by two academics, Julian Lim and David F. Dinges, concluded – what I am sure you already know – that a lack of sleep slows down your ability to think and function. Another study by researchers at Finland's University of Turku found that sleep deprivation makes it harder to maintain your focus and attention.
- Failing to exercise appears to be as damaging to your productivity as having a few sleepless nights, with research showing a clear link between work performance and how much physical activity you take part in. Thankfully, you don't need to spend hours running or lifting weights at the gym – a 2016 workplace study found you can improve work productivity simply by spending more time standing up while working.
- You might be a light eater, choosing to occasionally fast and be happy to 'run on an empty stomach', but if you don't eat appropriately and consume enough water, your ability to work productively will decline. A 2011 study in *Perspectives in Public Health* found that by improving your nutritional intake, you can raise your productivity by 2 per cent, while 2015 research in the *British Journal of Health Psychology* found a clear link between the amounts of fruits and vegetables you eat and your levels of positivity and engagement in your work and creativity.

Sleep and rest well

Ask yourself, what will it take for you to wake up refreshed, positive and full of energy? Do you need a full eight hours of sleep each night? Do you need to get to bed earlier, change your bedroom curtains to keep out the street lights or stop checking your emails before falling asleep to ensure you aren't kept awake by worrying about work problems?

Try using one of the many smart watches and related apps available, which can help monitor your sleep patterns and make helpful suggestions about how you can improve your quality of sleep.

Have an exercise plan and stick to it

Think about what you need to do to make the time and space to regularly undertake your preferred fitness activity or sport. No matter whether you simply like taking a daily stroll, doing morning stretches, training for half marathons or swimming 100 laps at your local pool – make regular time in your daily schedule and just do it! You could even seek out a health and fitness coach to help you select the most appropriate activities based on your current level of fitness and physical make-up.

Eat and drink optimally

Clean up your diet and eating habits by exploring what you need to change to improve your physical and mental health. Try reducing your alcohol intake and avoid consuming too many carbohydrates. Instead drink more water and eat foods that are proven to increase your brain power such as oily fish, nuts, avocadoes and eggs.

Look out for later chapters where we'll explore the need to maintain other aspects of your health, such as your mental and emotional health – all of which are essential in maintaining your productivity.

SAY 'NO'

You can't be all things to all people all of the time!

Sometimes you just have to stop being so nice. You may think you're being super productive saying 'yes' every time you're asked to do something – after all, it creates much less friction compared to pushing back. It might even make you popular. But there's nothing impressive about building up an impossibly long to-do list just because you can't say 'no'. At some point you'll either fail to deliver what you've promised or you may even find yourself suffering from burnout. Think carefully before you:

- agree to complete a report by Thursday, when you know the only free time in your diary is in the following week
- put up your hand in a team meeting to lead a project, when you're certain it will overwhelm you and your work schedule
- say 'yes' to working over the weekend to finalize some budget numbers, knowing you have family events lined up.

It's far better to complete a few tasks well than to struggle with a long list that will leave you overloaded and stressed. Productive people know this. They've mastered the art of setting boundaries and learning to say 'no' when necessary.

Understand yourself

Ask yourself why you find it hard to say 'no'. It will probably come from your natural desire to be helpful and liked. This is not unique to you – we all want to be loved, to go along with other people's needs and to avoid the tension that comes from saying 'no'. The secret is to learn to balance this need with your own realities. There simply aren't enough hours in the day to please everyone.

Pause before answering

It may help if you pause before responding to requests. Don't reply to that email straight away, and get comfortable saying 'I'll come back to you' in a meeting. Give yourself time to review your schedule and to-do list so you can decide if you are able to take on the additional work.

Set boundaries

Your door cannot always be open. It might help reduce your sense of guilt if you respond with facts. Share your schedule or your to-do list. If you really feel obliged to help, try negotiating. Suggest taking on only a part of the task or propose a deadline that fits with your own work schedule.

PRIORITIZE

Sort out what is important and what is urgent – and ignore everything else.

If you only rely on the opinions of your boss and the people you work with, it's likely that every single task will be both urgent and essential. As far as your colleagues are concerned, you should be dancing to their tune, not yours:

- 'I need this report by this afternoon, so please pause everything else and get onto it.'
- 'Please finish this important task today, as it's super urgent.'
- 'Drop everything else and please edit this report, since it's for the big boss.'
- 'You must complete this review by Friday, because it's the most important item in next Monday's management meeting.'
- 'Sorry we didn't ask earlier, but the client needs you to reply to them by close of play today.'

Of course everybody has the right to tell you that their needs are special, but it's your right to filter them through your own lens. Successful people pro-actively manage what they're working on, determining the different levels of priority for each task. As they are passed new and often unexpected requests to do things they'll constantly weigh up the importance and urgency of each request, and will re-order their to-do list accordingly.

They will typically use an urgent versus important matrix which is also re-ferred to as an Eisenhower matrix. This tool requires that all your tasks are placed into one of four quadrants on a table (shown below) based on the extent to which each is task urgent or not urgent, and important or not important.

important but not urgent	important and urgent
neither important nor urgent	urgent but not important

Chapter 6

Use the Eisenhower Matrix

Take a moment now to place each task on your current to-do list into one of the following four quadrants. Once you have placed each of your to-do list tasks into a quadrant, apply these rules:

Tasks that are both important and urgent

These tasks should receive your highest priority and need completing now. They require your attention and focus, and if there are many tasks in this category, you may need to rank them to decide which to focus on first and for how long.

Important tasks that are not urgent

These tasks also need doing, but they can be de-prioritized. Just because they are not urgent today though, avoid the mistake of putting them on the back-burner and then either forgetting about them or rushing to complete them at the last minute. The ideal is to plan ahead and schedule time in your calendar for focusing on these important tasks.

Tasks that are not important but are urgent

Since they're not important, try to get them off your own to-do list by asking yourself if you could delegate them. If you have to complete them yourself, think about how you might minimize the time and effort you invest so you have more time and energy for your more important unfinished tasks.

And finally, tasks that are neither important nor urgent

Try to ignore these tasks and delete them from your to-do list. If they do need completing, pass them to more junior colleagues, outsource them to others or even try to automate them. Whatever you do, spend as little of your time on them as possible. Chapter 8 contains more advice on how you can eliminate trivial tasks.

KNOW WHEN TO SWITCH OFF

You're not a long-life battery – you will run down eventually.

Continually being in work mode can have horrible consequences on your productivity and quality of life. If you spend every waking moment thinking about work, taking phone calls, checking emails and messages, it will inevitably take its toll on you.

In 2019, the Myer-Briggs Company surveyed over 1,000 people and found that those who had more difficulty switching off from work exhibited higher levels of job stress, lack of work–life balance and inability to focus on one task at a time. Out of all the respondents who admitted to being unable to stop working:

- 28 per cent said they were unable to mentally switch off
- 26 per cent admitted that work interfered with their family and personal life
- 20 per cent reported being mentally exhausted.

Switching off means letting go and recovering your sense of balance and calmness. It means using time to focus on non-work stuff, emptying your mind of work pressures and getting a good night's sleep so that you wake up energized, relaxed and ready to face the day. The alternative is a slow but inevitable decline in energy, motivation, positivity and productivity leading to eventual burnout.

Don't take work home

As hard as it might seem, you need to find a balance between performing your job well and taking time out to re-charge. This might require some changes to your working style. If you commute to and from an office, decide how you are going to use your travelling time. Could you commit to using your commute to switch off from work completely? Or could you compromise and work on the commute but commit to never doing office work at home?

If you regularly work from home, you need to set boundaries between your working and non-working space and time. If possible, have a workspace in your home that you can physically step away from, ideally with a door that you can close. Always leave your laptop, work phone and papers in your dedicated work area. Try to mentally leave your work head there as well when you step away.

Whatever you do, try to establish a regular pattern of work and down time each day.

Create 'switching off' ground rules

If you really need to work outside of office hours, you might keep one weekend day work-free and allocate a couple of work hours on the other. Maybe you could instigate a 60-minute rule on weekday evenings for clearing important emails.

Whatever you do, avoid working on your laptop or phone just before falling asleep or as soon as you wake up. You just won't perform at your best at those times. Oh, and holidays? Don't even think about it.

ELIMINATE THE TRIVIAL

Stop leaking energy and time – leave personal distractions at home.

If you're wasting time on trivial and useless tasks, you're not alone. Research shows this is a common problem:

- A McKinsey Global Institute study found that only 39 per cent of our time is spent on tasks that are specific to our job role.
- A 2018 survey of 3,000 people in eight countries by Kronos Corporation found that 9 out of 10 respondents wasted time by focusing on activities unrelated to their core job, with 41 per cent saying they lose over an hour a day on non-essential tasks.
- Vouchercloud.com asked nearly 2,000 UK-based office workers how long they thought they spent working productively in a typical working day. The average answer was only 2 hours and 53 minutes.

So what are we all doing when we're working so unproductively? The answer is a mix of trivial personal and work-related tasks such as:

Personal-related	Work-related
Gossiping with friends and family	In unnecessary meetings
Browsing and shopping online	Wading through unproductive emails
Day dreaming	Re-doing or replicating work
Job-hunting	Completing reports no one reads

This is a masterclass right here in what *not* to do if you want to be productive. Productive people not only avoid these distractions, they work out as a matter of priority how their time *is* being consumed. When you know that, you can eliminate all the useless stuff and, at the same time, leave the personal/non-work to-do list at home.

Chapter 8

Do a waste audit

Take an honest look at yourself to understand where you might be leaking time and energy at work. Refer back to the 'urgent versus important matrix' (Chapter 6) and detail those trivial tasks that sit in the matrix's two quadrants for unimportant activities.

To help make your list, observe how you spend your working day. Take a note of when you spend time on activities that don't deliver value. These are tasks that would have no negligible impact on your work success if you completely ignored them.

Eliminate the waste

For each task you'll need to decide how to proceed. You might simply ignore them, hoping no one else notices. You might delegate, or agree with your boss to have the tasks removed from your area of responsibility. You'll find advice and tools throughout the book on how you can shed parts of your workload.

Evaluate non-essential tasks

We can all be guilty of doing personal tasks when we should be working, whether it's a bit of harmless web-surfing, a dash of online shopping, some social networking or a bit of speculative job-hunting. Every minute you spend on these activities is a minute less invested in your work. It's up to you to decide if that's a good trade-off.

Whatever you choose to do at work, just be honest with yourself about the impact that your non-essential and non-work tasks have on your ability to do your job well and achieve your goals and targets.

KNOW IF YOU'RE A MORNING OR EVENING PERSON

Are you a night owl or a morning bird? Work when you feel most
alive and energetic!

Blame your ancestors for whether you're a morning or evening person. A 2019 research study, published in the journal *Nature Communications*, concluded that it is your DNA that determines your circadian rhythm or natural sleep-wake cycle, and this in turn predisposes you to be more productive and alert at different times of the day. This is why we all have different energy patterns. Morning people are most productive and mentally sharp before lunchtime, while evening people get going later in the day. If you're at your peak late in the evening, you're probably a night owl.

Knowing when you are most alive, energetic and productive is important as this is the best time for you to do the bulk of your work, particularly the demanding tasks that you need to be mentally alert for. Unfortunately, many of us have to work at times of the day when we're not at our best, for example working across time zones, night shifts or irregular hours. Forcing your mind and body to be active at times that don't fit with your circadian rhythms can be detrimental to your health and productivity. Research published in the *Journal of the US National Institute on Alcohol Abuse and Alcoholism* found that disturbing your normal sleep-wake patterns can lead to depression, alcohol dependency and psychiatric disorders.

Not everyone is lucky enough to get to pick and choose, but highly productive people will generally stick to their natural preferred circadian patterns, taking care to rest and recover when they're forced to break them.

Chapter 9

Know your natural pattern ...

Bear in mind that it's not always obvious what your natural sleep-wake cycle is. You may *think* you're a morning person simply because your lifestyle or job demands that you get up before 6am. The reality is, you might be much more productive in a role that starts and finishes later in the day.

To find your natural pattern, experiment and observe how you feel when working at different times of the day. Be aware that we do change over time, with research suggesting that as we age, we gravitate to being earlier risers and less alert in the later afternoon and evenings.

... and work with it, not against it

When you are confident of your natural cycle, always book important meetings or do your most challenging work when you know you're at your best. I'm a morning person so I prefer to kick off any important discussions and brainstorming sessions by 9am. One of my business partners is the opposite and pushes critical meetings to the middle of the afternoon or even early evening.

Make use of any available flexi-time arrangements at work to the extent of starting early and finishing up after lunch if you are strongly a morning person. Likewise, delay the start of your day and finish up in the evening if you're a night owl. Hopefully this will be one of the benefits of the increase in home-working – the flexibility to adjust your working day.

Make the most of the power nap

A quick power nap at an appropriate time of the day can help you maintain your performance, so if you're a morning person don't be shy about taking a short rest in the early afternoon to help you get through the rest of your working day.

SHARE THE LOAD

You're not superhuman – if you need help, ask for it!

Trying to do everything yourself is a pretty common habit and you might do this for all kinds of reasons:

- You want to show the boss you can do it by yourself.
- You decide it's quicker to write the report yourself than find a colleague to do it for you.
- You don't trust a team member to be an effective stand-in at a meeting.
- You think asking for help is a sign of weakness.
- You are a bit of a control freak and not comfortable involving others.
- You can't be bothered with the hassle of explaining to someone else how to complete the task.
- You don't trust any of your team to complete the task on time.

These justifications may be perfectly valid, but you'll never reach maximum productivity if you hold onto everything yourself. By holding onto these beliefs, you will:

- miss the opportunity of working on different tasks while others are helping you
- take on work yourself that other people might do better than you
- risk becoming overwhelmed and burnt out.

You don't have to be an expert at everything and it's fine to accept your weaknesses. Productive people know they're not superhuman. They'll always try to share their workload by asking for help, delegating tasks and supporting and thanking those who help them.

Understand why you won't let go

Using the list on the previous page as a prompt, think about times you've opted to complete tasks alone, and the reasons you've used to justify that. Be honest with yourself and don't feel embarrassed or guilty. If you don't trust your colleagues or like having all the glory for yourself, it's ok.

Be willing to ask for help

Decide which items on your to-do list could be completed by other people, and which you absolutely have to do yourself. Once you've done that, think about who the right person would be to pick up the slack. At work it might be your team members, peers, boss or a supplier. At home it might be your partner, children or friends. Take the time to explain why you need their help, and be grateful and positive if they're willing to dive in. Be sure to show your thanks by offering to help them in return. If someone's too busy to help you, be understanding and don't make them feel bad.

Teach and trust

Take the time to mentor, train and teach people who are helping you, showing them what's required to successfully complete the tasks. Be patient and trusting, accepting they might make mistakes, particularly if the task is new to them. Don't over-react when they're slow or struggle. Remember and appreciate that they are doing you a favour by trying to help you, so don't be too harsh if they don't do a perfect job.

Avoid common delegation mistakes

When you have your own team, avoid demotivating them by giving them too much to do and only giving them tedious or boring tasks. Be conscious of workloads and mix up the quality of work. It's really important to steer clear of showing favouritism by consistently delegating the interesting or easier tasks to the same people.

BECOME TECH SAVVY

The future is digital.

It's impossible to get anything done without technology. We'd be lost without our laptops and smartphones. Organizations would grind to a halt if staff couldn't access systems, databases and files on the Cloud.

Being smart with technology is an essential skill and a study by the consulting firm McKinsey came to the same conclusion. Published in 2021, their study, 'Defining the skills citizens will need in the future world of work', concluded that to be successful you need to master four skill sets. The first three are 'self-leadership', 'cognitive/thinking abilities' and 'interpersonal skills'. The fourth is called 'digital skills' and is broken down into three parts:

- **digital fluency and citizenship** which covers how to learn and collaborate online
- **software use and development** which covers being able to analyse data, understand some software coding and the algorithms that underpin them
- **understanding digital systems** which embraces skills such as systems thinking, cybersecurity, data analytics and being able to translate needs into tech solutions.

For maximum productivity, there's no way round it, you need to get tech savvy. Use technology to increase your efficiency and take advantage of every tool at your disposal.

Chapter **11**

Embrace digital skills

Being productive doesn't mean becoming a tech geek, but you do need to be aware of and willing to learn about digital skills. Make a conscious decision to give them the same focus and attention you give the other skills and competencies you've mastered in doing your job well.

Start with a goal of being more tech savvy than the people you work with by:

- embracing any tech tool, system or device that can help you perform even better
- learning about technological innovations, solutions, services and products that may impact your organization
- making time to read articles, learning from technology-fluent colleagues and visiting conferences and expos
- being the first to explore and experiment with new digital solutions.

In Chapter 85 you'll also be encouraged to embrace artificial intelligence (AI) and to find ways it can help you boost your productivity.

DO WHAT YOU LOVE

Be a passionate performer!

To succeed in life, do what you love. I'm sure you've heard this before – it's the basis of numerous self-help books and motivational speeches, with Steve Jobs' 2005 address to Stanford University students being one of the best-known examples.

There's a reason this idea is popular – because it's true! Common sense says that if you enjoy doing something then you're more likely to do more of it, to do it better and to become expert at it.

Science supports the link between passion and performance, with much of the research based on the idea of being 'in the flow' – a concept that was developed in the 1970s by the University of Chicago's Professor Mihaly Csikszentmihalyi. His research found that when you're doing work that you love, the work feels effortless and highly motivating, and your performance improves because:

- tasks are easier to undertake
- you have increased confidence
- you have greater energy
- you feel more positive and optimistic
- time passes faster
- repetitive tasks are less tedious or boring
- you persist and focus
- you find challenges less difficult.

Some people are lucky enough to work in fields they love, often because they're following a childhood passion for animals, aircraft or design, for instance. If this is you, you have probably experienced being in the flow.

If not, don't despair. Most people work in jobs they weren't pre-disposed to love, but we can all *learn* to love what we do. A 2015 University of Michigan study published in the *Personality and Social Psychology Bulletin* found that to be successful and highly productive you don't need to feel 'love at first sight' with any new job or career move. Instead, your passion can be cultivated and grown over time as you build experience and expertise.

Find your passion ...

Make a list of what you love, listing the kinds of work and tasks you really enjoy and maybe even feel passionate about. It may not surprise you to hear that I love writing and helping other people. Your own list might be a combination such as leading, making, teaching, driving, creating. Feel free to include particular professions or sectors such as law or the software industry. If you struggle to produce a list, try writing down the type of work you *don't* enjoy.

... and work at it

If you're not already working in a job that aligns with what you love, ask yourself what else you could do. If you want to make a career change, plan out how you'll pull it off. You should include a realistic timeframe and list the key actions, which might include acquiring new skills, finding a career coach, or identifying a mentor who is already working in the field you want to move into.

If you're in a job you don't feel passionate about, make a conscious decision to thrive and be successful despite everything. Bring a determination to excel to your work. Learn as much as possible and find ways to successfully complete all of your tasks.

IT'S OK TO BE IMPERFECT

Don't let fear of failure destroy you.

Good news for perfectionists. You're likely to produce the best outcomes, out-perform your colleagues and over-deliver for your clients. An extensive 2018 review of 95 studies, reported in the *Journal of Applied Psychology*, found that perfectionists tend to be more engaged, motivated and willing to work longer hours than their colleagues.

So, if perfectionism is so great, why is it OK to be imperfect? There are three reasons:

- Perfectionists may be paying too high a price. The same study found a strong correlation between perfectionism and higher levels of depression, stress, burnout, anxiety and workaholic tendencies.
- The extra time perfectionists invest may have little impact on their work's quality. They might be setting excessively high standards that are neither expected nor valued by their bosses or clients.
- Overall performance can suffer – by devoting more time to every task, perfectionists are likely to miss deadlines and fall behind in completing the rest of your to-do list.

If you want to be a perfectionist, research says be an excellence-seeking one, rather than one who works long hours for fear of failing. Research published in the journal *Personality and Individual Differences*, studied both types of perfectionists and found that those who work hard for fear of failure are much more likely to see their productivity decline and ultimately face burnout.

Chapter 13

Manage your perfectionism

Be selective about where you allocate your time. There'll always be tasks where a higher level of perfection is needed. Spend the extra minutes, hours or even days on these tasks but learn to distinguish what needs the extra mile and what doesn't.

The secret is to do this selectively and not to allow your perfectionist tendencies to become addictive and something you apply to every piece of work. Over-working will only wear you out and you'll become stressed from missing deadlines.

Try time-boxing

To help you control how long you spend on each task, try time-boxing. This involves you deciding how long you'll spend on something and then sticking to it. With each task, choose a sensible amount of time based on your experience of how long you'll need to complete it well but not 100 per cent perfect. As with the Pomodoro technique, set a timer and once it rings quickly wrap up what you're doing and treat it as finished.

When you're working with others, have them hold you accountable by asking them to check in with you at agreed times to see if you've completed a task you're working on. If you find yourself saying something like 'I just need a little more time to make it even better', get them to challenge you. You might find you've already completed it to an acceptable degree.

Treat your addiction

If you can't shake perfectionism, you may need to treat it as an addiction and be ready to seek therapy or counselling from a professional skilled in eliminating addictive habits.

DON'T PROCRASTINATE

Putting off today until tomorrow only makes today easier.

Getting started on new tasks is hard. Sometimes it's just a question of being overloaded, but other times it's procrastination, which is a much bigger problem. We're all guilty of it. We've all opted to delay doing something important, even though we know that a hold-up will have negative consequences. That's a simplified version of the definition of procrastination that was created by the academic Katrin Klingsieck. It goes without saying that being a procrastinator is not helpful to work performance.

Procrastination isn't productive or healthy. One study by the University of Calgary's Piers Steel concluded that it impacts our lives in more ways than you would expect, including:

- performing poorly at work
- feeling bad about yourself
- missing out on opportunities
- delaying medical care
- overpaying for purchases.

So if we all know procrastinating is bad, why do we do it? There are a few different reasons:

- a lack of motivation or drive so you lack the energy to get started
- feeling depressed, anxious or stressed, which can immobilize you
- knowing or thinking the task will be too difficult
- finding the task boring, tedious and dull
- not liking the task or feeling you won't enjoy doing it.

Productive people never allow any of these reasons to stop them getting started, no matter how boring, difficult or unknown the work may be.

Chapter **14**

Just start!

If there's something big you're avoiding doing, just getting started is a great way to break the procrastination cycle. Research shows that once you've started a task, you'll come back and complete it. It doesn't matter how long you work on it, just get going and ignore any negative feelings associated with it.

It might sound too good to be true, but there's a well-researched psychological reason why 'getting started' will help you overcome procrastination. It's known as the Zeigarnik effect which is a tendency for unfinished or interrupted work to be much more prominently remembered than tasks that have been completed or never commenced. So in other words, once you've started, even if you've only done a very small amount of work, the need to complete it will play on you, bringing you back to finish up.

Once you've done this a few times, you'll find it's easier to get started on tasks that you used to avoid doing.

Work on your mindset

Getting started works, but try to create a more positive and healthy mindset too:

- Continually look for enjoyment and motivation in your work and avoid dwelling on the negatives (this links to the idea in Chapter 12 of being in the flow).
- Don't allow your work to make you feel moody, stressed or anxious.

By doing this you'll be better placed to face tasks which in the past you might have avoided, because a positive and energized mindset sets you up to take on any challenging or tedious work.

SLEEP ON IT

'If only I could take back what I wrote in that damn email!'

Communication may seem like a strange topic for a book on productivity, but an ill-judged comment or a message sent in error can easily have a negative impact on your performance as well as your relationships.

You put a lot into building those connections, and the trust between you and your colleagues is the oil that makes the engine work, reducing friction and allowing you to perform at your best. An ill-judged comment can bring down the whole house of cards in a moment, whether it's just a sarcastic aside in a team meeting, or a reply to a client that was intended for a colleague. It's becoming increasingly common for social media posts to cause problems too. I've seen career growth stalled or even terminated because of poorly thought through social media posts.

Reputations can be made or broken in an instant so make sure that you are as careful with your communication as you are with your to-do list. Your productivity will stall if your communication isn't up to scratch.

Take time to cool off

Productive people know that pausing to double check what they want to say can be the difference between performing well and losing out on a project or promotion.

All of your communication should be clear, relevant and understandable. And unless you've got very specific reasons, it should never be demotivating, upsetting, accusatory or over-reacting.

Stick to the golden rules:

* Whenever you reply to a message, make sure you've understood the preceding message chain. Speak with someone if necessary to clarify before responding in writing. It can make the difference between a thoughtful and appropriate response or one that shows you haven't bothered to understand what other people are saying.
* If someone says something that upsets you, keep your mouth closed and fingers away from your keyboard. The likelihood of you saying the wrong thing is really high when your blood is boiling. Wait until your emotions have cooled down before responding (or don't respond at all).
* When you want to be sure that your message is ideally worded and presented, do a practice draft, save it, then step away. Come back later to re-read it and decide if it's good to go or needs editing.

KEEP YOUR WORKSPACE TIDY

A tidy desk may not mean a tidy mind – but it does make it easier to find things.

You know the saying, a tidy desk is a tidy mind? It seems to be true:

- In a 2019 study, published in the journal *Building and Environment*, researchers found that the physical environment, including how tidy and organized it is, significantly impacts your thinking abilities, emotions and quality of your interaction with other people.
- A tidy work area is better for your physical health, particularly in the post-COVID-19 era, since it's a lot easier to clean and sanitize a desk and work area that's free of clutter. A cleaner work area will help you stay healthier.
- A messy workspace could even be the cause of stress. Research in the US journal *Environment and Behavior* established a connection and found that it's two-way. Stress may cause you to neglect your workspace which in turn increases your stress levels.
- And finally, people you work with may view you negatively if they associate you with a messy workspace. In one 2019 study, in the journal *Personality and Individual Differences*, people who had messy offices were perceived by their colleagues as less agreeable and conscientious.

It's time for a Marie Kondo-style declutter, so roll up your sleeves and get stuck in. You may not enjoy it, but think of the benefits for your productivity.

Chapter 16

Get organized

Make it part of your daily or weekly to-do list to keep your workspace clean, organized and structured. Invest in a filing system for your physical documents and paperwork so that you and your colleagues can easily find things.

You should also keep all of your digital files well organized (we'll explore this in more detail in Chapter 73).

Create a shared workspace policy

If you share a workspace and colleagues are happy with the mess, you'll need to talk them round to your way of thinking. Get everyone to agree to a simple set of rules for keeping the common work area uncluttered for everybody's benefit.

Break the tidy rule

There is one good reason to have a messy office though, and that's to fuel your creativity. This is borne out by research, including a paper from 2013, in the journal *Psychological Science*, which concluded that people in messy rooms were more creative than people in very orderly rooms. This might justify having a messy space set aside for creative work, or allowing your work area to be left disorganized specifically to support creative bursts and then tidied up again afterwards.

LEARN FROM SETBACKS

When you hit a wall, take out your sledge hammer.

Productive people know how easily a setback can stop them in their tracks. You might be working productively right up until the moment that something blocks your way – but it doesn't matter how smartly you've worked on something if you don't actually complete it. I've heard of so many stories of people giving up, even when working on things that mean so much to them:

- The newly hired designer who presented what she believed was a really creative new product design to her colleagues. They responded very critically in the meeting, demotivating her and causing her to give up on her idea.
- A friend who had two jobs in order to build up enough savings to put down a deposit on a new apartment, but the housing market was so active he kept missing out on having an offer accepted. He became so frustrated he decided to continue renting.
- The daughter of a neighbour who studied hard throughout her degree course only to fail some of her final year exams. Instead of retaking them after the summer break, she walked away from her degree.

We all become annoyed, angry and frustrated when our plans hit a wall. At this point, when other people might give up, productive people pause to assess their situation. They tap into their reserves of determination and persistence and continue working towards their goals.

Of course, sometimes, giving up can be the optimal decision, but only if it's clear that continuing will be fruitless and success is no longer possible. Your challenge is to decide if this is the case, or if the urge to stop is simply because you're upset and frustrated.

Avoid hasty reactions

When one of your ideas is criticized, or your draft work fails to impress, it's very easy to give up. You'll feel angry and upset and in the heat of the moment it's natural to want to walk away. Pause, allow yourself to calm down, and only when you're in the right frame of mind, decide if, and how, you wish to continue with that particular activity or piece of work.

Treat setbacks as learning

Being productive involves evolving and developing over time, and when you struggle with any task, ask yourself: 'What can I learn from this rejection, failure or criticism?' Explore what it would take for you to succeed. You might need to change focus, involve others or use different thinking, tools or processes to help you perform well.

Be persistent

Some people just seem to have a mindset that means they never give up. Whether it's inherited or developed over time, they find it much easier to continue with their work no matter how many obstacles and setbacks they may have faced. If that's not you, don't worry. You can train yourself to become more determined and persistent. Try these approaches:

- Continually remind yourself why you want to succeed with a difficult task. Visualize the benefits of completing the work, and always keep in mind your purpose for completing it.
- Have someone hold you accountable. Ask a colleague to support you by checking in on your progress, and give them permission to challenge you when you are considering giving up.
- Take a break from the task to positively re-energize yourself. Mentally step away from the frustrations you might be feeling. Your break could take the form of actual time off work but it could just be turning your attention to simpler tasks for a bit.

USE EACH DAY WELL

Life is short, and a single day is even shorter!

Working long hours each day won't make you more productive. This was confirmed in a 2019 *Harvard Business Review* reported survey of 20,000 people, which concluded that working longer hours doesn't translate into higher levels of individual productivity. Productive people already know this, and instead of planning to spend 18 hours a day at work, they plan how they'll spend each day in a smart way.

The same study found that highly productive people have three daily habits in common:

1 Each working day they create a daily to-do list.
2 They manage well all information flows during the day.
3 They make time for other people.

These daily habits correlate with other studies and the advice of successful people, with the consensus being that to be productive you need to have:

• a daily plan for how the working day will be spent. This avoids the risk of time being wasted and used inefficiently, including being pulled in different directions by other people's needs
• a number of productive daily routines that create clarity and certainty, and give structure to the working day.

Best practice routines include:

• immediately completing any important tasks that will only take a couple of minutes (which is sometimes referred to as the 'two-minute rule')
• ensuring there is time for breaks and lunch, as well as time to exercise at certain times of the day
• structuring the day optimally, for example having all face-to-face meetings in the mornings and leaving afternoons free to focus on paperwork and emails.

Write a plan of action

Make a daily plan part of your routine. It's up to you when you do this. Some people prefer completing it at the end of the previous day, others prefer to make it their first task of the morning. Just before drafting it, take time to review what you achieved in the previous day and what's still pending or unfinished.

Your daily plan is more than simply a to-do list of tasks. It should also help you break down your working day, so that you have sufficient time allocated for:

• your super-important and essential tasks
• unexpected and unplanned requests for your time – this might include blocking a couple of hours each day for important and urgent requests that you typically receive from your boss, colleagues or clients etc.
• your important routines and preferences for how you want to spend each day, including time for your well-being – exercise, eating, relaxing and reflecting etc.

Include one key task

As a rule, plan time each day to complete at least one really important task, or part of a longer key task. Getting this done should be very motivating and the highlight of your day.

Decide if each day is the same as the next

Think about whether certain days of the week should be treated differently and have their own specific daily action plans. For example, many productive people use their Mondays and Fridays in the following specific ways:

• **Monday:** Given it's the start of the week, Monday might be spent allocating time to catch up with team members and colleagues to review the week ahead.
• **Friday**: You might use the last day of the week to catch up on emails, make phone calls or read articles and reports that have been building up in your inbox.

See Chapter 76 for more on task-batching.

MANAGE YOUR EMAILS

Develop healthy email habits for optimum productivity.

When you're not sitting in meetings, I bet you spend most of your time reading and responding to emails. The number of emails we have to deal with is staggering and, given the volume, it's no surprise that we spend hours every day reading and writing them:

- One recent UK survey of 1,500 people by Pure Property Finance found that on average we have 651 unread emails in our inboxes.
- Every day each of us on average receives 121 work emails and sends out 40 according to 2019 research quoted in the UK's *Guardian* newspaper.
- A 2018 survey of 1,000 people by Adobe found that on average people spent over three hours a day on emails. This is already a large percentage of the working day, but the same survey found that people spent over two hours a day on *personal* emails too.

Spending so much time on emails isn't only time-consuming, it's also unhealthy. In widely cited research by UC Irvine and the US Army, researchers using heart monitors concluded that when someone spends time away from their emails, they experience significantly less stress and are better able to focus.

Given how much of our time and energy is spent emailing, it is only logical that if you want to work productively you have to make sure that you're working smart and have healthy email habits.

Develop good email habits

A McKinsey study found that on average we check our email inboxes every 37 minutes. This can be very disruptive since you'll be constantly switching between other tasks and checking your emails. Try limiting your inbox visits to once every two or three hours.

The following hacks will help you develop good email habits:

- **Read selectively**: try reading only the titles of unread emails to determine which ones you really need to open. Then make a further call on what needs to be read in detail and what can be skimmed. You might also decide that for emails where you're only a cc a quick skim is enough.
- **Limit time spent writing emails**: challenge yourself by asking whether picking up the phone would be quicker than writing a reply. Question whether you need to 'reply all' and whether you need to reply at all when you're only a cc or bcc.
- **Decide if your emails need filing**: think about inbox management. Are you happy with a single large inbox where you rely on your email system's search function to find what you're looking for or do you need a filing system that you can easily return to?
- **Make best use of your email system**: whatever email system you're using, be sure to use whatever functionality is available. Ask IT support colleagues for advice and tips.

START WITH THE HARDEST TASK

Your first task of the day sets the stage for how productive you'll be later.

You have a choice every morning when you start your working day of whether to tackle the easiest and quickest wins first or jump into your most challenging and important task. Most people choose the easy wins, particularly given the feel-good factor that comes from being able to quickly tick things off your to-do list.

This habit of doing the easy things first is known as 'task completion preference' and sometimes it's ok to do, but often it's not a productive choice. In Harvard Business School published research from 2019, busy ER doctors were found to focus on the quicker tasks first, which in their case were patients who were the least ill. As a result, the more seriously ill patients, who required more of the doctors' time and expertise, had to wait longer. By the time doctors got to them, they would often be tired and not at their best.

Highly productive people start each day by doing the most important and hardest task in front of them. No matter how challenging, boring or difficult, this is the task they'll work on first. Having clarity around how they'll start each working day also helps them avoid procrastinating about what to do first.

Chapter 20

Tackle the important tasks first

Using the 'important-urgent matrix' you learned about in Chapter 6, rank your day's to-do list items into important and not important. Then start the day by focusing on completing the single most important task on your list. If you have two or more equally important tasks, start on the one that appears to be the hardest.

Tackling your most complicated tasks at the start of your day means that you'll bring fresh focus and energy to them. If you leave them until later, you may struggle to finish them before going home, which means you'll miss out on the feel-good factor that comes from completing them.

Start with warm-up

You may be reluctant to jump into such a big task. In this case, a quick warm-up on some smaller tasks is ok, but only for a few minutes. Examples of quick tasks might include checking your email inbox and having a quick daily team meeting.

To be sure that these quick tasks don't grow in size and distract you from getting started on the big task, be firm and only allocate the first 30 minutes to your warm-up. Then spend the remainder of your morning on your hardest task.

TO BURN OR NOT TO BURN THE MIDNIGHT OIL

Be aware of the dangers of living on the edge.

How rock 'n' roll are you? If you like to do everything at the last possible moment and rush to meet deadlines and targets, you're probably getting an adrenaline rush from living on the edge. According to scientific research, this can give a heady dose of adrenaline as well as higher levels of the so-called happy hormone, dopamine.

It's no wonder that some people literally become addicted to starting every task when it's almost too late. This isn't simply procrastination, it's a conscious choice that surprisingly does bring with it a couple of benefits:

- By the time you start the work, you're more certain that it actually needs doing. There's nothing worse than completing a task early only to discover it's no longer required or that the requirements have changed.
- If you start a task early, you're likely to spend longer on it which might improve quality but you'll have wasted more time. Whereas the later you start, the less time you'll have to devote to it and the less time you'll waste. This is known as Parkinson's Law.

These benefits might be real, but so are the potential downsides of a last-minute working style:

- You might run out of time and miss deadlines, or have to rush and impact quality.
- You might enjoy the adrenaline and dopamine highs, but your body and mind might not and could be negatively impacted by the resulting stress.
- You might undermine the work of your colleagues if your contributions are always arriving at the last minute.

We all have unique working styles depending on our personalities. Some of us like to finish tasks ahead of time, while others always leave things until the last moment. Productive people are aware of the advantages and disadvantages of both and rather than having only one way of working, they vary their style depending on the situation.

Assess the risk

If you're a last-minute sort of person, only do it with your easy and well-known tasks – those pieces of work that you're super confident you can start close to their deadlines and complete well, without any risk of being delayed or of producing poor quality.

For brand new, more complicated tasks, or for those you're not sure how long they'll take, always start working on them as soon as possible. This avoids the risks of either running out of time or having to produce a rushed piece of work.

Work backwards from deadlines

When creating or updating your to-do list make sure you show any requested deadlines, and think through how long you need to complete the work, bearing in mind factors such as:

• the level of complexity
• the need for other people's inputs
• the degree to which it's a new task
• what can go wrong
• the benefits of finishing earlier than expected
• the risks and penalties of being late or not meeting quality expectations.

You can then work backwards from the deadlines to determine when you need to start working on each task, adding some buffer time in case you need more time than you estimated. Your to-do list template might look something like this:

Details of task	Expected time to complete	Start date (or time)	Deadline

KEEP MEETINGS EFFECTIVE

Your time is precious – guard it fiercely.

When asked about meetings at work, most people talk about them being too long, boring, disorganized or badly run. Research confirms that many meetings are a waste of time.

- In a 2019 survey by the US headhunting firm Korn Ferry, 67 per cent of respondents claimed to spend so much time in face-to-face and virtual meetings that they were unable to perform their other tasks well.
- A 2014 study by management consultants Bain & Co., summarized in the *Harvard Business Review*, concluded that senior leaders spend two full days per week in meetings and that dysfunctional meeting habits and behaviours are becoming more common.
- Professor Steven Rogelberg at the University of North Carolina has studied meeting effectiveness, and in the MIT *Sloan Management Review* states that only about 50 per cent of all meetings are effective and engaging.

There are so many reasons why meetings can be unproductive:

- They're too long.
- It's unclear why they're being held.
- There are too many attendees.
- There are no written agendas.
- Attendees don't know why they've been invited.
- Certain people dominate discussions.
- People in the meeting get distracted.
- Discussions go off topic.
- There are no follow-on action plans or minutes.
- Incorrect people attend.
- Nobody prepares beforehand.
- There are too many PowerPoint slides.
- The meeting chair fails to control discussions.
- No conclusions are reached or actions agreed.
- Attendees don't listen to each other.

With the increase in working from home and online meetings, there are the additional challenges of poor internet connectivity impacting the quality of many meetings as well as many attendees leaving their cameras turned off which makes it harder to engage and connect together.

Decline meeting invitations

Be ruthless in managing what you put in your diary. Never simply accept meeting invitations, even when they're from your boss and other senior colleagues. Evaluate the pros and cons of attending any meeting you're invited to, saying 'no' to the invite when you feel your time can be better used in other ways. The email calendar invite might give you enough information to make a decision. If not, check with the meeting's organizer to learn more, asking them why they've invited you.

Demand quality

Productive people recognize ineffective meetings and avoid all unnecessary ones, while ensuring that those they do attend are as well organized as possible. When you're organizing a meeting, you can personally ensure it'll be well planned and run. As an attendee of other people's meetings, you can also make suggestions to help ensure each meeting will be as productive as possible. Here are some key best practices to follow and to request of any meeting chair:

- Have a clear and written meeting agenda which states the items to be shared, presented and discussed, and who will lead each item and for how long.
- The agenda should be circulated beforehand to all invited participants.
- Have a clear reason why each invited person needs to attend.
- Ensure the meeting is chaired in such a way that all ideas and opinions can be raised and discussed openly.
- Have ground rules such as no multi-tasking in the meeting, the importance of listening when others are speaking and not interrupting each other.
- Ensure the length of any meeting is optimal (Chapter 47 explores this in more detail).
- Have a written set of minutes and/or an action plan prepared and circulated afterwards (this is explored in Chapter 70).

WORK TO YOUR STRENGTHS

What use is a sundial if it's in the shade?

Highly productive people work in fields that utilize their strengths rather than forcing them to rely on their weaker skills. Given a choice, we all prefer doing things we're good at and which make use of our strengths. Who wants to struggle to complete tasks that don't use their talents? Extensive research by the US company Gallup has found that this strengths-based focus helps people perform better and is also less stressful and more motivating and engaging.

Unfortunately, many of us never think about what we are really good at and we never find work that'll capitalize on our natural and acquired strengths. Instead, we spend years working in jobs that require us to develop and use skills that we may not naturally possess at all.

As an example, I once knew an accountant who kept making mistakes with calculations. It was a couple of years later that she admitted she wasn't cut out to work in finance and book-keeping and that her talents lay in other areas, such as in communicating with people. She moved roles within her company and became very successful in the customer service department, rising to lead the entire team. When mentoring new hires today, she shares her story and encourages her younger colleagues to always try to work with their strengths and natural talents.

Identify your strengths

Before being able to use your natural and acquired talents, you need to recognize what they are. A quick way to discover them is to ask those you live and work with what they perceive as your strongest qualities and traits. Invite them to be as open as possible.

In addition, you could try taking one of the many online personality or skills assessment tests which are focused on uncovering your main strengths and talents. Some of the better known such assessments are:

- Wingfinder by Red Bull
- Strength Deployment Inventory
- HIGH5 Strengths Test
- Clifton Strengths Assessment.

Develop new strengths

As you grow your career and win job promotions, you'll need to develop new strengths to help you deal with the new responsibilities that come with each role. As well as nurturing and sustaining your existing areas of expertise and talent, you may need to work on specific skills which you may have neglected or never even considered developing and using.

Work with others' strengths

Be prepared to seek the help of other people, particularly when they may have strengths you don't possess. For example, if you're not a details-oriented person, try delegating any editing and proofreading of important documents to a colleague whose strength and experience lie in that area.

Don't obsess about your weaknesses

Understand and accept where you might be weaker. There's really nothing wrong with having areas where you're unskilled, inexperienced and lacking in talent. If these unused and weaker skills aren't needed to help you become more productive, let them go and stop obsessing about them. Focus instead on growing those skills you really need to develop to help you achieve success.

THE POWER OF REPETITION AND RITUAL

We are the sum of what we repeatedly and consistently do.

We're all creatures of habit. We thrive on predictability and repetition, and each of us has our own rituals such as watching the same TV shows, having coffee breaks with the same colleagues, eating the same food on particular days of the week or taking the same weekend walks. Repetition helps ground and comfort us, giving us some sense of control in our ever-changing world.

You can become more successful if you focus on repeating helpful and productive activities, habits and actions, while avoiding those which will have the opposite impact. Examples of things a productive person might choose to repeat include:

- getting up early each day to meditate
- exercising every morning
- having 'me-time' each day to recharge
- reading a book for a few minutes every day
- having a break from emails and technology at weekends
- having a positive word with your colleagues every day
- preparing well for every meeting.
- eating healthy food everyday

It's no major hardship repeating habits that are easy and feel good, such as starting every day with a healthy fruit juice, ignoring your inbox at the weekends or reading a self-help book every evening. What's more challenging is repeating productive activities that require effort and can seem tedious and boring. It can be hard to find the self-discipline and commitment to do activities such as:

- writing up your notes after every meeting
- keeping your emails and documents filed correctly
- updating your to-do list at the end of every afternoon.

Highly productive people know that we become what we do each day. They'll make sure to find the commitment to repeat the right habits and activities no matter how time-consuming or boring they seem.

Chapter 24

Develop good rituals

Take a look at how you spend your time to identify the things you repeat on a daily and weekly basis, from the moment you wake up through to going to sleep at the end of the day.

Make a list of these habits and activities and for each one, ask yourself to what extent the ritual makes you feel good and positive, how healthy it is for you and in what way it helps you to become more productive.

Aim to eliminate those habits that make you less productive, recognizing that this will take more effort with those habits that you enjoy doing but are ultimately unhealthy, unproductive and/or time-wasting.

Commit to repeat healthy habits

Once you've got your list of healthy and productive habits and rituals, your challenge is to commit to repeat them on a regular basis no matter how tedious, time-consuming or boring they may be. Don't allow any excuses such as being too busy or not feeling good to stop you.

Motivate yourself with the thought that once you start regularly repeating any habit, then over time that habit will become easier to do. It will take less effort as it becomes automatic and second nature.

KEEP A PRODUCTIVITY JOURNAL

Learning happens when you write it down.

In your drive to become more productive and successful you'll experiment with all kinds of productivity hacks, including trying out the advice in this book. Some days you'll succeed in being more effective and efficient while on others you'll struggle. Only by taking the time to write it all down will you be able to remember and learn from your efforts. If you don't take notes you'll quickly forget what worked well and what you didn't like, such as:

- how you broke down a large task into smaller and more manageable parts
- how you quickly completed a difficult task
- how you convinced a reluctant colleague to help you with your work.

Keeping notes in the form of a journal helps you remember what you did, and it can also improve your brainstorming and decision-making skills. In one piece of research by Ball State University in the USA, and published in the *Journal of Athletic Training*, researchers found that keeping a journal was an invaluable tool for exploring past experiences and actions, while drawing insights to help with your future challenges.

Writing about your daily activities can also help improve your time management skills, which are a key aspect of being productive. As you write about your daily work experiences you'll start noticing patterns about how you're spending your time which you can address. You might spot, for example, that you're not completing as many of your to-do list items as you hoped, or a certain type of task is always taking you longer than planned.

Find a method that works for you

If you've always enjoyed keeping a written diary, then beginning to journal about your work is a simple extension of your daily writing habits. If on the other hand this is all new, it's ok – you don't need to write pages upon pages of journal reflections each week. Just making a few notes on a daily or weekly basis is enough. You can write or type and do it wherever is easiest for you – in a special journal or notebook, in your diary, on your PC or on your smartphone.

To help structure your written reflections, here are some questions that you could reflect upon each time you write:

- What tasks did you complete today/this week, and how well did you complete each of them?
- With each task, what did you learn or realize when working on it?
- What productivity tools and hacks did you use and how helpful were they?
- With hindsight what could you have done differently to be more productive?
- During the day (or week), when were you at your most productive and when were you at your least, and why?
- How did you cope with any unplanned urgent requests and other interruptions?

FINISH WHAT YOU START

Be clear about what you have started – and keep going to the end.

We all have different preferences about the kind of work we enjoy doing. Some of us enjoy getting started on new tasks while others love seeing things through to the end. When you think about yourself and those you work with, you'll recognize these two common working styles:

The Starter ...	The Finisher ...
... loves exploring how to undertake tasks and being the one who plans what needs to be done.	... is happy to be asked to spend time working on any task, even when that entails some quite repetitive work, with no end in sight.
... is eager to commence work on tasks and is really proud of what they've achieved even when the work is only half completed.	... is motivated to work on anything until the very end, and really proud to have completed a task.

The most common mistake people make is to be a starter and not a finisher. They work on tasks but step away before actually finishing anything, preferring to jump to new projects. Research by University of Chicago psychologists Ayelet Fishbach and Minjung Koo found that this tendency of starting but not finishing things is caused by people who have a premature sense of fulfilment. This is caused by focusing too much on what they've achieved to date rather than being motivated by what's left to be done. Finishers tend to be less easily distracted by success to date and instead remain focused on what still needs to be done to fully complete the task.

It goes without saying that to be a highly productive person, you need to be an all-rounder ready to adopt whichever combination of the two styles is needed to successfully complete each piece of work.

Know yourself

Observe yourself in action to discover how much of a finisher you are. Ask your colleagues for their feedback and observations about your pattern of starting and finishing tasks.

If you're still not sure of your pattern or if you simply wish to delve deeper into understanding your preferences, complete a widely available personality test called the Belbin Team Roles. The results will show you your working style preferences, including the extent to which you are what the assessment tool refers to as a 'Completer Finisher'.

Reassess your priorities

When you find your attention being drawn away from an important task, pause and take time out to reassess your priorities. You could do this by reviewing your to-list as well as reminding yourself of the importance of the task that you're not finishing. If the unfinished task remains important, find ways of compelling yourself to spend time on it until you've completed it. You might try:

- asking a colleague or family member to hold you accountable – they could check in with you each day or week to understand how well you're progressing on it
- switching off all other distractions such as notifications on your PC and blocking your calendar
- working from home or from another work location where you don't normally work – this will help you focus on the task at hand by making it harder for your colleagues to find and disturb you.

TO MULTI-TASK OR NOT TO MULTI-TASK?

Productive people resist the urge to multi-task, and are single-task focused.

Multi-tasking might make you *feel* productive, giving you a sense that you are successfully completing many of your tasks at the same time, but it will kill your performance. Extensive research shows that it is extremely unproductive compared to focusing on completing one task at a time. This is because of the inefficiencies that come from switching between tasks, particularly when the tasks are complicated and different.

The most famous research on this topic was published in the *Journal of Experimental Psychology* by three researchers who claim that multi-tasking can reduce your productivity by up to 40 per cent. Their research showed that as we move back and forth between unrelated tasks, we have to first turn off and then turn on different cognitive rules for how we complete them, a switch which is inefficient and time-wasting. Other studies reach similar conclusions:

- A Stanford University study from 2009 showed that multi-taskers are more mentally disorganized and that they struggle to switch between tasks.
- Multi-tasking on your devices might even be bad for your brain functioning and health according to 2014 research by the University of Sussex.

Even if you agree that multi-tasking is inefficient, it's hard to avoid doing it. In recent years thanks to streamlining and cost-cutting we all seem to be busier in our jobs and are expected to achieve more with fewer resources. Productive people aren't immune to this and there's a natural temptation to multi-task, but the most successful people resist it and remain single-task focused.

Chapter **27**

Multi-task with extreme care

According to David Strayer at the University of Utah, about 2 per cent of humans are what he calls super-taskers. In extensive research these rare individuals have the cognitive abilities to multi-task without any decline in their performance. If you are such a person – lucky you. Keep doing what you're doing. If you're not, be very careful about when and where you juggle more than one task at the same time.

Move from multi- to single-tasking

Recognize when you are being pushed to work on multiple tasks at the same time. Note in your weekly and daily to-do lists those requests that have similar deadlines for completion. Put them into a logical order for completing them, ensuring you work on only one task at a time. If you must move between tasks, don't do it every few minutes but only once or twice a day.

You might feel you enjoy switching between tasks and it may even have become an addiction. I see this in my coaching work when a person is talking with me but cannot stop checking their phone for emails or messages. If you are guilty of this, find ways to remain focused on a single task:

- Turn off your phone or PC while reading and editing the hard copy of a long document or attending an important meeting.
- Close browsers, apps, notifications and programs when working on your computer on a key task, to stop your attention being pulled to other things.
- Hide away in a meeting room where no one can find you to avoid being drawn into other tasks by your colleagues.

TAKE A BREAK FROM YOUR PHONE

Smartphones can be our greatest friend – and our worst enemy!

Blame it on dopamine, but everyone seems to be addicted to their phone. Passengers on public transport glued to them, pedestrians bumping into you because they're walking and scrolling at the same time, even car drivers messaging while driving.

Many of us are constantly using our smartphones because our brains push us to engage in pleasure-seeking activities, such as checking our social media posts for comments and likes, sending and awaiting replies to messages and searching online for answers. There's even a name for a person's fear of not having accessing to their smartphone: nomophobia.

Research confirms what you'd guess – you cannot be productive if you bring a smartphone addiction to work with you.

- Time-wasting is a big problem. One survey of over 1,000 people by Screen Education found that an average employee spends over two hours a day accessing digital content which has nothing to do with their work.
- The same study found that 14 per cent of survey respondents knew of at least one accident, which was sometimes serious, caused by a colleague being distracted while using their smartphone.
- A Florida State University study in 2015 showed that simply receiving a notification of a message on your phone is enough to significantly reduce your ability to focus on your work.
- Even when your phone is on silent or switched off it can distract you from your work according to a University of Texas at Austin study published in the *Journal of the Association for Consumer Research*. Researchers found that simply by being within your reach, your phone can be a mental distraction.

Turn it off

From a productivity point of view, the ideal behaviour is to leave your phone at home when you leave for work, or if you're home-working leave it switched off far from your working area.

But this is impossible for most of us. Mobile phones have become the main way of communicating with each other – from your child's school calling you in an emergency to a colleague sharing urgent news with you. On top of that, we're increasingly expected to work on our smartphones, whether it's answering emails, attending Teams meetings or being on your department's WhatsApp group. So, if you cannot hide your phone or leave it switched off, try the following productivity hacks:

- During important meetings or when you want to avoid non-essential distractions, switch off internet access by putting your phone into aircraft mode. You can still receive phone calls and SMS messages, but you're minimizing other distractions.
- Go 'old school' and use a non-smartphone at work so you don't have internet access or connectivity.
- Turn off notifications and your phone's sound, unless you're 100 per cent certain that you really need to see any messages as soon as they're received.
- Remove social media and other distracting apps from the phone you use at work.

BREAK DOWN LARGE TASKS

Be like a climber of Mount Everest – start at base camp and move
on from there.

Sometimes your goals and aims are simply too large and too complicated to
tackle all in one go, and it's logical to break them down into smaller and more
manageable pieces. Each of these smaller tasks serves as a step towards your
larger overall goal. This is highly productive because breaking down any large
task into smaller parts will simplify the work, making it ...

- ... less daunting. Aiming to reach the summit of Mount Everest is a pretty
  daunting prospect. But when the task is broken down into its individual
  components – moving from camp to camp before aiming for the summit –
  it becomes more achievable. The same thinking can be employed with any
  large goal.
- ... more mentally manageable. Our brains cannot work on a task that is too
  complex given that the part of our brain that we use for mental tasks is limited. According to 2010 research published in the journal *Current Directions
  in Psychological Science*, it can only remember three to five items. With a
  large and complicated task it can be so hard to understand what has to be
  done and to visualize how the task will be completed.
- ... more motivating. By breaking down a task into more manageable goals,
  you're able to celebrate regular 'wins' as you complete each of these smaller milestones. You can imagine climbers celebrating their arriving at each
  of Mount Everest's camps on their way to its summit.
- ... more efficient. Productivity experts agree that breaking down tasks into
  smaller deliverables is the most efficient way of completing the work. You
  can better plan and allocate resources, including time and people, to each
  smaller task. This is both logical and core to today's project management
  best practices, including agile and waterfall principles.

Become expert in task planning

With any goal or task, decide if it'll be easier and more productive to break it down into smaller deliverables, or if it should remain as one single task. To determine the answer, you'll need to understand what is needed to complete the overall task in terms of complexity, resources, processes and outputs. For example, the goal of creating this finished book breaks downs into a number of very different tasks – from agreeing the book's focus, to creating the structure, drafting the content, editing and proofreading it, typesetting and printing it, and then distributing it to bookstores and making it available for sale online.

As a rule of thumb if a task requires a long time and involves a range of processes and people, then it should be broken down into smaller parts.

Map out smaller tasks

You'll need to decide if the range of smaller tasks and deliverables needs to be completed sequentially or can be undertaken simultaneously. A useful tool to help you map out the timeframes for each of the different tasks is a Gantt chart. These charts list the tasks on the vertical axis and intervals of time on the horizontal axis. For each task you can show the time period it'll take to complete.

EMBRACE ERGONOMICS

Invest in the right equipment for optimum performance.

Most of us have experienced the back aches, throbbing wrists or tired eyes that come from spending too long working in an uncomfortable chair, looking down at your PC screen and using a keyboard at the wrong height. You're very lucky if you've never had any of these symptoms because most equipment and furniture isn't as healthy and comfortable as it could be. It's not ergonomically efficient – ergonomics being the field of study focusing on the impact of and appropriate design of our living and working environments.

There is extensive research showing that working with the wrong equipment and furniture can be bad for your health and productivity. One extensive study, published in the *Journal of Safety Research* in 2008, analysed 250 different case studies of the impact of improving a workplace ergonomically, for example through providing better chairs, tables and computer screen heights. The study's conclusion was that these improvements led to:

- reduced work-related musculoskeletal disorders
- fewer sick days and health insurance claims
- a fall in staff turnover and absenteeism
- an increase in productivity.

It's a productivity quick fix to invest in a more suitable office chair, light or table and it will be repaid quickly through better health which in turn leads to improved performance.

Chapter 30

Upgrade your work area

The most important piece of equipment is your office chair and having an ergonomically friendly one can have a massive impact on your health and performance. Choose a chair that:

- is adjustable so that you can choose the height of the seat so that your feet are flat on the floor, your thighs horizontal and your arms are in line with the height of the desk
- has good lumbar support for your lower back as well as supporting your upper back and neck
- can swivel so that you can move around without straining yourself.

If possible, also use an adjustable-height desk so that when sitting with your feet on the floor your arms can comfortably rest on your desk. Sometimes you might raise your desk to allow you to alternate between standing and sitting. The importance of standing to improve your productivity is explored in Chapter 61. In addition to your chair and desk, you should:

- ensure that your computer screen is at your head height, so that you don't have to look up or down and risk straining your neck
- have a separate keyboard which sits on your desk, along with an ergonomic mouse to help avoid straining your hands and wrists
- optimize your lighting in your work area, and ensure that your computer screen is free of any glare which might strain your eyes.

STOP OVER-PROMISING

Don't offer more than you can deliver.

No one likes it when a friend or colleague commits to doing something by a certain time and they forget, do it badly or finish later than promised. When this happens, you're left feeling like they don't care, they're lazy, inefficient, unproductive or even untrustworthy.

It's so important for your success to meet expectations and be seen as a reliable person who does what you say you're going to do. It doesn't matter how productive you are in other aspects of your work, breaking your promises can lead to lost business, strained relationships and even damaged careers.

You don't even need to exceed expectations to be successful, but you must at least meet them. This was confirmed in 2014 research published in the journal *Social Psychological and Personality Science*, in which UC San Diego and University of Chicago academics concluded that breaking one's promises is very costly, but that exceeding them brings little benefit.

Think of this in terms of arranging a delivery to your home – you are expecting it at a certain time and you plan for that. You'll be very annoyed if it's late, but may not be particularly grateful if it arrives early.

So rather than aiming to under-promise and over-deliver, start by simply ensuring you do what you say you'll do, never coming in late or at lower-than-expected quality levels.

Chapter 31

Avoid saying 'yes' when you mean 'no'

Avoid the tendency to agree to timeframes or workloads that you know you cannot meet simply to avoid having a difficult conversation. It's better to be honest today by pushing back than to affect your reputation later when you miss a deadline which you knew you couldn't meet.

It's ok to beat what you promise by a small amount. It shows you are working well while also setting reasonable expectations. Don't go over the top though. If you repeatedly beat deadlines and timeframes by large margins it'll confuse people who will conclude either that you're playing games or there's something wrong with your planning.

Set win-win promises

When negotiating deadlines, be open with your boss or client about the basis and assumptions behind your calculations. You may want to be very open by sharing how much slack or buffer is included in your estimate.

If you're not sure how difficult a task will be to complete and you are unable to give a definitive timeframe, be open about it. You could commit to complete the work as fast as possible while also agreeing that you'll check in regularly to review progress.

FOLLOW THE TWO-PIZZA RULE

If you have to shout in a team meeting to be heard, then your team is too large.

When working in a team, you'll struggle to be productive if the team is too large. There's no magic size, although Amazon's founder Jeff Bezos is credited with saying that you should limit the number of people in any team so that they can be fed with two pizzas.

Depending on how greedy and hungry your team are, anywhere between about three and twelve people would be happy with a couple of pizzas, and these numbers correlate with the most quoted researcher in this field, the late J. Richard Hackman. Working at Harvard, he concluded that for most tasks the optimal team size is six and that no team should exceed ten. When it does, performance issues are likely to grow exponentially. Other research on team size by Caroline Aubé, Vincent Rousseau and Sébastien Tremblay came to a similar conclusion, finding that small teams experience better work outcomes.

Most people who've worked in any kind of team are likely to agree that it's easier working with a smaller group of people than a larger group. The positives of smaller teams include:

- quicker to share information
- easier to have discussions
- every member knows their colleagues well
- decision-making is more efficient
- fewer people leads to fewer disagreements and conflicts
- team meetings can be shorter and more to the point
- easier for the team leader to work with each person
- fewer people to create camps and sub-groups
- easier to hold each team member accountable since no one can easily hide away.

All of these examples of the positive impacts of being a small team link to improved productivity and team performance. This is why you must always be careful when leading or creating a team to ensure you get the optimal size.

Chapter 32

Understand the team's needs

When you're part of, or leading, a very large team – say 15–20 people – don't treat this group as you would a smaller one. Things will be different, starting with the fact that you may not be able to bring everyone around a single meeting table to get things done. Much of the face-to-face communication with the team may look and feel more like a town hall meeting.

In these situations, be on the lookout for and willing to address issues that arise because of the team's size. These can easily have a detrimental impact on the team's overall performance, as well as your own. Common examples include:

- It takes more time to share or gather information from everyone.
- One-on-one catch-ups may happen less frequently.
- It can be difficult to know all of your colleagues really well.
- It can be challenging to remember who does what, in terms of roles and responsibilities.
- Collective decision-making and implementation can be slower.
- There may be tensions, disagreements or conflicts between team members.
- Team meetings can be long if everyone's inputs are being sought.

Create teams within your team

Just as we spoke of breaking up large tasks into smaller ones in Chapter 29, if you're leading a very large team, break it up into smaller sub-groups. These sub-groups of six to ten people can be tasked with specific work and left to operate as optimally sized teams with their own appointed team leaders who report to you. These teams will hopefully be free of the inefficiencies that can arise when a team is too large.

SET SMART GOALS

A vague goal is nothing more than wishful thinking.

The key to successful productivity is being clear about what you need to achieve and ensuring that any goal you set yourself (or others) is as clear and detailed as possible.

You've probably heard the saying 'If you don't know where you're heading, how will you know when you've arrived?'. This is how it can feel to pursue goals that are too simple and vague, compared to goals that are more structured and detailed. The following examples demonstrate this point:

Goals expressed very simply	The same goals re-stated in more detail
Let's land astronauts on Mars.	This year let's start developing the necessary technology and people capability to have a first manned mission to the surface of Mars, to land on the planet within ten years.
We wish to grow our business.	We wish to grow our company size by 500 per cent (in terms of revenue) over the next four years, through exploring new markets, opening a new manufacturing plant and expanding our online offerings.
I want to develop my tech skills.	In order to optimize my performance and career opportunities, I'll spend the next week mapping out precisely what technology-related skills and knowledge I need to master and then I'll find the ideal training courses and learning tools.

A simply worded goal can be very useful as a vision or purpose to rally people behind your message or cause. NASA might well announce that it wants to land astronauts on Mars, but to make this happen they'll need a more detailed and comprehensive goal, with supporting sub-goals. These more detailed goals should be designed as SMART and CLEAR goals.

Chapter **33**

Turn all goals into SMART goals

A SMART goal is one that is specific, measurable, attainable, realistic and timely. Starting today whenever you create goals, plans and aims, ensure they're SMART.

- **Make them Specific** – the goal should be written in a detailed and clear way so that everyone can fully understand what is expected. When creating goals for a team to work together, make the wording of the goal as specific as possible.
- **Make them Measurable** – ask yourself how you can accurately measure the goal to monitor if it is being achieved. It'll be easier to create measurement metrics if the goal is objective and factual rather than being vague and subjective.
- **Make them Attainable** – ensure any goal you set can be achieved, since there's little value in setting yourself or others goals that are unattainable. To do so is both demotivating and probably a waste of time.
- **Make them Realistic** – realistic goals are similar to goals being attainable; your goals should be sensible, relevant and realistically related to your work and areas of responsibility.
- **Make them Timely** – you need to set realistic targets for when a goal will be completed. By having deadlines, you can continually assess if you're either ahead of or behind schedule and make the necessary adjustments.

Although this goal-setting process might seem a little complicated, once you start creating goals in this way, it'll become easy with practice.

ENSURE GOALS ARE PURE AND CLEAR

Clear goals lead to higher success.

In today's fast-changing and agile world we're all being encouraged to act more sustainably, more ethically and be more purpose driven. This should be reflected in the goals that you set for yourself and other people. In order to reflect these expectations in your goal-setting, in addition to being SMART, your goals should be both PURE and CLEAR. These goal-setting-related acronyms were created by the late leadership coach and author Sir John Whitmore.

Making your goals PURE helps ensure you are creating goals for the right reasons, and when stated as PURE your goals should be positive, understandable, relevant and ethical:

- Being **positive** means the goals are aimed at creating a positive outcome rather than one that is based on avoiding something bad happening.
- Everybody involved in working towards your goals must be able to clearly **understand** them.
- As well as being realistic, your goals should be **relevant** to what you and your team are skilled and trained to do.
- Working towards and reaching your goals should never involve challenging you or anyone else **ethically**.

Stating your goals as CLEAR ensures they are acceptable to those impacted by the goals being achieved. The goals should be challenging, legal, environmentally friendly, agreeable and recorded:

- In order to motivate and help you and your colleagues grow, your goals should be **challenging**.
- Just as any goal you set should be ethical, it must also be **legal**.
- Your goals should be **environmentally friendly** and not cause any resources to be wasted or for the environment to be negatively impacted in any way.
- If you need the help of others to achieve your goals you must ensure that they **agree** with the goal and how it can be achieved.
- Productive people always make sure that their goals are written down and **recorded** to enable anyone to refer to them as needed.

Ensure your goals are PURE ...

- **P**: Make sure that your goal positively describes whatever it is that you wish to achieve, as opposed to describing something you wish to avoid. As an example, it's better to say you want to create an excellent report that is well drafted and perfectly written than to state that your goal is to create a report that contains no errors or mistakes.

- **U**: To ensure that relevant people understand your goal, share a draft with them and have them describe what they understand. From their responses, you'll know if your goal description is a bit unclear and may need revising.

- **R**: Think through what abilities and resources will be required to complete the goal's tasks and ensure that anyone working on it, including yourself, has what they need to succeed.

- **E**: Ensure that the goal can be reached without needing to break rules, cut corners, cheat or lie.

... and CLEAR

- **C**: Recognize that when a goal is not challenging at all it might be very boring and demotivating to work on, whereas a goal that is too challenging might have the opposite impact.

- **L**: It's important to ensure that your goal doesn't involve anyone having to break the law to achieve it. Ask the advice of other people, including a lawyer, if this is a possibility.

- **E**: With any work-related goal, it's important that achieving it has as little negative impact on the environment as possible. Any goal should be worked towards in the most sustainable and carbon-neutral way possible.

- **A**: The easiest way to find out if your team or colleagues agree with a goal is to ask them and to listen well to what they have to say.

- **R**: Think through how you'll write down and record details of your goals. This might be in the minutes of a team meeting, in an email sent to colleagues or shared in an online collaboration tool.

NEVER AVOID THE SHITTY WORK

Value your work – both the good and the bad – and always do your best.

It can be very tempting to be selective about what you do and to avoid the stuff you don't like. It's only human to want to work on things that interest, excite or motivate you, while ignoring the more tedious, repetitive or boring bits.

This is fine if the work you're avoiding can be completed by other people or forgotten about – but there'll always be something important that only you can complete:

- re-filing or indexing a large amount of printed or online materials that you've created which others struggle to understand
- editing a long report which your colleagues would find it very difficult to do given its complicated content
- inputting a large amount of data into an online system when no one is available to help you.

Productive people have a consistency about how they approach their work, recognizing that all important tasks must get the same attention and focus no matter how interesting or boring they appear. They'll prioritize their time and focus based on the value and importance of each task on their to-do lists and never on how fun or interesting they are.

This changes slightly when you look to the longer term, so steering a course towards working on things you are passionate about and developing plans and budgets to enable you to delegate, automate or eliminate work you find boring, tedious or repetitive is fine. It just has to be balanced with the priorities in the here and now.

Get started

There's a lot of wisdom in the words 'just do it'. When facing a large pile of dirty dishes waiting to be washed or hundreds of pages of a document that need editing, you can either ignore the work and face the consequences, or get stuck in.

If you jump into tasks with a positive mindset and focused attention, you'll be surprised how easily you'll forget how boring or repetitive you imagined the work would be.

Do it well

Not enjoying a task is no excuse for completing it without care and attention. With dull or unpopular tasks, it can be tempting to cut corners, to rush and not to bother checking your work. Yes, you may have quickly cleared those tasks off your to-do list, but you're not working in a highly productive way.

Delegate and outsource

The obvious solution with any task you'd rather avoid is to find another way of getting it done that is both smart and workable:

- When the work is within your area of responsibility, always try to complete it at least once. This gives you an understanding of what the task entails and how it can be done well.
- You can then decide if you can delegate or pass it to others, which might involve you training or mentoring somebody. Work together if necessary and you could get it finished in half the time.
- You can also explore how these tasks and their related work processes might be outsourced, automated or at least reduced so that there's less so-called shitty work for you to have to focus on, leaving you more time for what you love. Chapter 46 explores the topic of automating processes.

WORK WITH THE 80-20 RULE

80 per cent of your results come from just 20 per cent of your work.

According to the Pareto principle, 80 per cent of your results come from only 20 per cent of your efforts. This could be 80 per cent of a company's sales coming from 20 per cent of its customers, or 80 per cent of a team's performance coming from the efforts of 20 per cent of the team.

Although the actual ratio will rarely be exactly 80 per cent and 20 per cent, the 80/20 principle or 80/20 rule shows that if you look hard enough, you'll always find examples of this imbalance between the time and effort invested and the results produced:

- 70 per cent of your team's ideas might come from only 20 per cent of the team members
- 85 per cent of your new customers might come from only 30 per cent of your cold calls
- 25 per cent of your staff might be responsible for creating 90 per cent of the error-free products
- 20 per cent of your social media posts might generate 80 per cent of the desired followers' reactions.

Recognizing that a small part of what you do can be responsible for producing the majority of your results is an important tool in your productivity armoury. You can use this insight to maximize your performance. You might explore questions such as:

- If only 25 per cent of my clients yield 90 per cent of my sales, is it productive to retain the remaining 75 per cent?
- If 30 per cent of my staff bring in 75 per cent of my results, how should I be training the rest of my team to emulate these high performers?
- What can I learn from the most productive 50 per cent of my working day that I might apply to the remaining 50 per cent?

Understand your own 80–20 ratio

Work out the 20 per cent of your effort that's producing 80 per cent of your results. Don't worry about the exact percentages, think about the small things you do that have the greatest results, or approach it the other way and identify where you're exerting a lot of effort but getting minimal outcomes.

One way to go about it is to look at the tasks you often repeat and that take up a lot of your time. You'll probably discover the following kinds of patterns:

- Business development: 15 per cent of your client marketing calls yield all of the new product orders.
- Meetings: only about 30 per cent of the meetings you attend are helpful and productive.
- Marketing: 20 per cent of your blog posts receive 90 per cent of your blog's likes and shares.
- Email management: only 20 per cent of your emails actually need reading and responding to.

Learn from your top 20 per cent

Think about how you can put more time into the most productive elements of your work and what you can scale back on. Through a combination of observing, taking feedback and reverse engineering, try to learn what your top 20 per cent tell you about your:

- most productive brainstorming sessions or team meetings
- highest performing team members
- most popular marketing campaigns
- most successful business development activities.

Determine what works well and you'll know what you should be doing more of, copying, repeating and/or replicating.

LEARN TO FOCUS

Technology is quietly killing productivity with distractions.

In a survey by Udemy Research titled the '2018 Workplace Distraction Report', 70 per cent of the survey's respondents claimed to be regularly distracted at work, with 50 per cent saying they're significantly less productive as a result.

By their very nature, distractions can be pleasurable and rewarding, but they can have a negative impact:

- They create stress and anxiety by causing you to fall behind, rush to meet deadlines and not have the time to produce the level of quality work you aim for.
- They waste your energy by causing your focus and attention to wander.

There are separate chapters in the book on avoiding smartphone and internet distractions (Chapter 28 and Chapter 75 respectively), but this chapter is specifically about the power of focus. Focus is an ability you can develop by increasing your ability to concentrate and pay attention. Maximizing your focus will give you huge productivity dividends. On the next page, you'll learn how.

Clear focus

Try restricting your focus to a few key intentions and goals. Warren Buffett is widely quoted as saying you should only focus on your top five goals and ignore everything else, and that your to-do list should only contain those items.

Use the following hacks to maintain your focus:

- **Take breaks:** take regular short breaks during your working day. University of Illinois at Urbana-Champaign research, published in the journal *Cognition*, found that we are able to maintain optimal focus on a 40-minute visual task only if we take a short break during the exercise.
- **Take care when working from home:** negotiate with your friends and family, asking for no interruptions when you need to focus undisturbed, and promising your undivided attention later in return. If you need silence to focus, then work alone in a room where you can close the door and not be able to hear any TV or radio playing, kids, pets and household appliances etc.
- **Practise 'focus-improving' strategies:** strengthen your mental attention span through optimizing your diet, exercise regime, sleep pattern and the ways you relax and remain calm.

LISTEN WELL

Most people hear – but they aren't listening.

According to research from Accenture, 64 per cent of working professionals find it difficult to listen well in today's work environments. This is a big problem because communication issues reduce productivity. If communication is unclear, you're likely to:

- misunderstand what you're being asked to do
- not fully comprehend what is happening
- misinterpret questions being asked
- misread the importance of a task
- be misinformed about how a colleague can help you
- read the wrong meanings into feedback given to you
- misinterpret someone's opinion about your work
- fail to understand or motivate someone who works with you.

The link between listening skills and work performance has been validated by extensive research, with one 2018 study by American academic Professor Norris Wise and published in the *Journal of Psychology & Psychotherapy* concluding that when listening skills training is offered to a group of people it increases their performance.

Poor listening can take many forms. I'm sure you know colleagues, family members and friends who are guilty of these common mistakes:

- They start speaking while you're still talking.
- They show little interest and play with their phone.
- They look around, instead of at you.
- They don't seem to want to respond to what you've just said.
- They stay silent and you've no idea if they've understood you.
- They ask you to repeat what you said because they were distracted.

You can use this correlation between listening skills and productivity to your advantage by role modelling, as you'll find out on the following page.

Chapter **38**

Role model being a great listener

Listening to someone else is a skill. With a little conscious practice you can become an expert and set an example for others.

- **Look at the person you're in conversation with:** Face the person you're talking to, maintain eye contact and give them your undivided attention. Don't stare as this can become off-putting, and in some cultures can be offensive.
- **Switch off and be in the moment:** Stop thinking about other things when someone is trying to tell you something. Concentrate fully on the other person and what you are hearing. By doing this, you'll have less free space in your mind for inner dialogue and unrelated thoughts.
- **Show that you're listening:** If you remain totally silent it can, ironically, give the impression that you're distracted and not listening. To avoid this, nod and say things like 'I hear you' and 'I understand'. Don't interrupt or talk over the other person as this is off-putting.
- **Clarify and paraphrase:** Once the other person has finished talking, make sure you've fully understood what they're telling you, either by paraphrasing back what you heard or clarifying it. Paraphrasing involves offering a quick summary which enables the other party to confirm that you heard them correctly. Clarifying involves double checking by asking questions.

MAKE TIME FOR YOURSELF

Find a little time every day to relax and recharge.

It can be hard to make time for yourself. Diaries get filled with meetings, sitting at your desk makes you an easy target for passing colleagues, urgent requests, messages and calls. Unless you make a special effort, you can get through the whole day without having any time alone. But 'me time' is essential for three important and interconnected tasks. It means you can:

• step back and reflect on your workload, goals and challenges. Time without distractions means you can take stock and review your to-do list and what is being asked and expected of you
• focus on work that requires deep reflection and concentration, the sort of work that can only be done well when you're alone and without any distractions
• pause to re-charge, rest and recuperate. During your working day, it can be invaluable to take a walk, close your eyes, meditate, exercise, do yoga or simply sit in silence. Leaders sometimes do this for a few minutes before important meetings or presentations to calm and ready themselves. One leader I coached described it as 'slowing down before speeding up' moments.

Having time alone can also improve your team's productivity. In a well-cited 2002 study published in the journal *Current Directions in Psychological Science*, US academics found that the results of a team's brainstorming were greatly improved when team members alternated between brainstorming alone and then together in the whole group.

Start time blocking

Block out time in your diary for 'me time' before other people spot that you're available and request your presence at meetings. Proactively plan ahead and block different times – you might start with blocking only two hours a week, but very quickly you should learn to block as much time as you actually need to be by yourself.

If your colleagues try to double book this time by inviting you to meetings, push back assertively and inform them that you're not free. If it's a really essential meeting with your boss or a key client, reschedule your 'me time' to another time in your diary.

We explored the impact of being a morning, afternoon or evening person in Chapter 9 and when blocking time for yourself, decide if you choose the times of the day when you're at your best or if you leave those times for your meetings and work involving other people.

'Me time' isn't only for your work

Use some of your 'me time' to re-charge. Having silent moments between long and challenging meetings to reboot is good. Don't feel guilty about taking breaks during your day. You'll be more productive and focused in discussions and tasks you need to work on afterwards.

PRACTICE, PRACTICE, PRACTICE

Practice may not make perfect, but it helps you move in that direction.

One of the fastest ways to become productive is by practising the tasks and skills you need to do your job well. This might mean anything from getting good at Microsoft Excel, chairing team meetings, through to speaking with clients, editing documents and designing new products. Everyone has a range of skills, behaviours and habits they need to practise in order to excel.

The idea that it takes 10,000 hours of practice to become expert at something has been debunked. The ideal type of practice isn't repetition, it's the quality that matters. You can achieve this by engaging in deliberate practice. This requires focused attention and involves repeating something in a mindful, purposeful and systematic way. For example:

- Notice how you react and respond each time you're in a tense conversation. This will improve your conflict management skills.
- Video yourself making key presentations and then review the recordings to explore how you can improve next time.
- Have a colleague observe you chairing a weekly team meeting to give you feedback on how you might improve.
- Monitor your success in making cold calls and tailor your sales pitch accordingly.

Deliberate practice is an important skill but on its own it won't guarantee you become a high performer. Research is showing that practising only partially explains the degree to which you excel at a task or skill. A 2014 study by academics at five universities, and published in the journal *Intelligence*, found that the amount of practice only explained up to one third of the difference in performance across a range of chess players and musicians. Other research is discovering that factors such as genetics, age, natural ability and how much you enjoy doing a task are also important. But deliberate practice *is* important and even if DNA is on your side, you're unlikely to excel at any task, skill or habit without it.

Chapter 40

Set time aside to practise

We now know that the idea that you need to practise an activity for 10,000 hours in order to master it is discredited, but you do need to continuously and regularly practise skills or tasks you want to master. This requires persistence, patience and determination to ensure you don't get lazy but instead put in the practice time you need.

You don't need to practise an entire activity. Just as a footballer might focus some of their training on corners, free kicks or tackling, and a swimmer might do drills to focus on a specific aspect of a stroke, you should also decide what skills, tasks or activities need to be practised deliberately and consciously to help you perform well.

Once you know what you want to practise, think through how to practise it mindfully, purposefully and systematically. This will depend on context and might vary between role-playing an activity before you perform it for real, visualizing in your head what you'll do in real life, or repeating an activity dozens of times while someone films you so you can watch it back later.

Getting feedback is really helpful, ideally from people who are already expert in the particular skill you're working on. Allow them to observe you practising and afterwards invite them to share their observations with you.

PLAN FOR THINGS GOING WRONG

Plan for the worst, but hope for the best.

When planning for victory in a road cycling race, professional teams focus on the obvious things they need to get right, such as having the fittest riders and the fastest bikes, but they also plan for the unexpected, such as how they'll handle mechanical and medical emergencies.

Productive people excel at 'what if' thinking. With any activity, task or project you should brainstorm the unexpected events that might derail progress and explore how these events might impact your performance. Once you have worked through what could go wrong, you should spend time thinking how you'd respond in each scenario. Some examples might include:

- Have a back-up source of internet access in case your main source fails.
- Do daily back-ups of your data and files.
- Spread risk by having many clients in case one stops working with you.
- Train more than one colleague in certain key skills in case one resigns or is ill.
- Build extra time into project timeframes in case of unexpected delays.

Just like the road cycling team who respond to their 'what ifs' by having spare bikes, a doctor and mechanics following their cyclists in support cars, you should give time to risk management and contingency planning. Productive people are never caught out when disaster strikes.

Chapter **41**

Stop being naïve

We live in an increasingly complex, uncertain and volatile world where the unexpected does often happen. You can't close your eyes to the possibility of a project being delayed, your expense budget being cut or a key colleague resigning with immediate effect.

The ideal mindset to adopt is to hope for the best while planning for the worst. If you're a naturally optimistic person this might take effort as you'll be inclined to focus on the positives. If you're naturally pessimistic you'll find it easy to think about what might go wrong.

Learn about risk management

Create a risk register. This is simply a list of the risks that you and your colleagues face. You can set it out in Word or Excel using separate columns:

- **Issue**: describe the nature of the problem.
- **Probability**: record your best-guess estimate of the probability of the issue happening.
- **Impact**: rate the issue in terms of the potential impact on you, your work and/or your organization.
- **Solution**: note the mitigation actions you are taking to minimize the possibility of this issue occurring or having a large impact.

For example:

Issue	Probability	Impact	Solution
The potential loss of data and information if my PC crashes and cannot be accessed	Low	High	I save all my files on the Cloud, as well as making weekly back-ups on an external hard drive. Later I will also invest in a second PC.

Regularly keep your risk register up to date and brainstorm the range of risks that might occur, especially looking out for any that might have been overlooked.

SEEK REGULAR FEEDBACK

Feedback is the fuel for your rocket of productivity.

Imagine living in a parallel universe where no one ever gave feedback – no one commented on each other's performance at work, or shared opinions on how anyone else is doing. In a zero-feedback world you might:

- complete your work incorrectly because no one warns you you're going off course
- become demotivated because no one gives you positive words of praise and encouragement
- misunderstand what others expect because you never check in with them
- chase the wrong goals because no one stops to tell you the right ones
- develop unhealthy work habits because no one gives you any developmental direction
- waste your time because no one warns you that you're not following processes.

You simply can't reach or maintain high levels of performance without feedback. This is supported by extensive research including:

- In 2020 research, published in the journal *Frontiers in Psychology*, German researchers found that when a person receives positive feedback, their self-efficacy increases, which means they feel more able to manage their own behaviours, emotions and motivations, which in turn enables them to be more successful at what they do.
- A 2013 survey of over 50,000 leaders, which was referenced in the *Harvard Business Review*, found that a leader's effectiveness positively correlated with their desire to obtain feedback about themselves.

Seeking as much feedback as possible goes hand in hand with high productivity. The best feedback often comes in the moment, such as asking a colleague how well your presentation went that day or how successfully you influenced your boss in a team meeting.

Chapter 42

Become a feedback junkie!

Don't wait for your performance review or until someone decides to give you constructive feedback. It's often too late by then. Seek out small amounts of feedback every day if possible. The secret is to ask people who have seen you in action and/or are impacted by your work and to ask them as soon as possible after the event.

- After a team meeting, ask the participants to rate the meeting and suggest ways you can improve the running of the next team gathering.
- When sharing a draft report or presentation, ask your colleagues for frank feedback about the document.
- If you're trying to strengthen a behaviour, such as your emotional intelligence (EQ), regularly ask how well you're demonstrating evidence of it (in this case, you'll want to know if you're showing improved self-awareness, self-control and empathy).

Instant, in-the-moment or even very recent feedback is valuable because:

- the feedback providers will be able to easily recall their opinions and feelings about you and your work
- you'll be able to connect any feedback to what you actually created, did or said
- you can immediately act upon the feedback to strengthen your strengths and to improve in other areas.

STOP PEOPLE-PLEASING

Don't say 'yes' to others if it means saying 'no' to yourself.

Emailing and messaging apps are a blessing and a curse. They mean we can all easily connect and share information, but the downside is that once you're on an email chain or added to a WhatsApp group, you're compelled to be involved in someone else's issues. Your challenge may not be the volume of emails and messages you receive each day, but the fact that many of them aren't addressed to you or even relevant to you. Being included means you have to decide whether to become involved or not. It isn't easy staying silent if someone's pulled you in. Many people jump in because they have something to say or their ego won't let them keep quiet. If you do this, you're wasting your time and energy.

There's a Polish proverb which goes, 'Not my circus, not my monkeys', or to be more literal, as a productive person would say, 'I'm not getting involved in your issues thank you very much'. For the sake of your productivity, avoid being sucked into work issues, challenges and requests that don't concern you or help you achieve your own goals. You can just ignore the communication, or query why you've been included and ask to be removed. Don't reply to everyone, just directly to the person who pulled you in.

The same applies when you're asked to get involved in a debate or argument, or attend meetings where the issues being discussed are of no relevance to you and your presence will bring no value.

Chapter 43

Develop a thick skin and push back ...

If you're a natural people-pleaser it can be easy to get involved in all the exchanges that come into your inbox and say 'yes' to all the meeting invites. It goes without saying that you need to push back. Start by observing how frequently you're being pulled into things that aren't core to your own work and note how you tend to respond.

Next time it happens, pause before jumping in. Skim the emails and meeting details, asking yourself if you need to be involved or could happily stay out. The answer is often obvious and it shouldn't take much thought to reach a conclusion.

When you know you should stay out but your habitual tendency is to join the debate, find the courage to break the habit. Don't overthink it. Instead, use the time you've saved for more important tasks. If you're challenged about why you never replied, just be polite but firm.

... but sometimes be willing to step in

There may be cases where it's good to become involved, even if it doesn't directly benefit you:

- to help and support your colleague(s) in debates and discussions
- to show you value them and to deepen your relationships
- to demonstrate that you're a team player.

EARLY TO RISE

Wake up early and seize the day!

Getting up early might be your secret to success. In 2020, the US bed manufacturer Amersleep surveyed and compared two groups of people – 510 early risers who get up between 4am and 7am and 506 late-risers who get up between 8am and noon. The early risers – particularly the 4am ones! – reported being more productive, had higher earnings and a better quality of life.

Setting your alarm earlier than normal brings numerous benefits:

- You're less likely to become distracted, as very few other people will be awake. When I get up around 5am there's a wonderful silence that helps me think and reflect.
- You can start your day in a calmer manner rather than rushing.
- Your brain and your willpower tend to be most alert in the mornings. This appears to be true even if you're not a morning person (you'll recall this from Chapter 9).
- You're more likely to get a better night's sleep according to research published in the journal *Chronobiology International.*
- It makes you more positive. 2014 research in the journal *Cognitive Therapy and Research* found that those who get up early have fewer negative thoughts than those who stay up late and sleep in.

Elon Musk, Tim Cook and Oprah Winfrey are all known for being early risers. Could you name any highly productive people who like a lie-in?

Chapter 44

Get up early

For the first few days of switching to getting up early it'll feel unnatural and difficult, but it will become easier. Even more so if you go to bed at a reasonable time and get enough hours of sleep. Eventually you'll get used to waking up early, no matter whether you describe yourself as a morning person or not.

Use your early mornings well ...

Experiment with how you use your newly found free time. It'll partly depend on your personality, interests and needs:

- Some people like to exercise by going for a walk, run, swim or to the gym.
- Others simply stay calm and meditate, read for leisure, stretch, do breathing exercises or practise yoga.
- There are those who jump into their workload, finding the silence enables them to think more clearly and focus on ticking items off their to-do list.
- And there are early risers who simply take things slowly, from having a long shower through to enjoying a leisurely breakfast.

Hal Elrod's *The Miracle Morning* is a great introduction to a structured morning routine.

... but be kind to yourself

Don't force yourself to work or do anything else just because you feel you should. Use these early hours in ways that motivate you and give you a positive start to your day. The key is that you're already up which in itself gives you an opportunity to have a more productive day, no matter how you spend your first few hours.

ASSUMPTIONS CAN BE DANGEROUS

No one ever suffered from too much clarity.

It always pays to check your assumptions. Misunderstandings about work – what's required, when it's required by – are all too common. It's easy for a minor misalignment around a particular instruction, timeframe, plan, expectation, request, agreement or question to derail a project and waste a lot of time.

Productive people are masters of double checking. Clarifying things up front might slow you down from getting started, but it means time well spent if it saves doing a U-turn down the line. So before you start your brief top-line report for the CEO, check what the expectations are. Before you write a proposal for your client, check that you have understood their brief. Before you drive to a meeting, check it's not online.

Assumptions can be dangerous and they have a habit of shapeshifting, convincing you to treat them as fact when they only exist in your head.

It's ok to sound stupid

Make sure you fully understand what's being asked of you when you agree to something. Ask clarifying questions or paraphrase what you've heard. It's always better to ask questions up front than to keep quiet and make a stupid mistake when completing the work. If it helps, ask the other party to confirm by email what they've verbally asked you to do.

Check in and seek feedback

If the task will take you a while or is particularly complicated, don't wait until you've completed it before asking for feedback. Show them a draft and ask them if your work meets their expectations and is in line with what you've agreed.

Learn from your mistakes

Take note of any times when you've made the wrong assumptions or heard something incorrectly and work out how to avoid the same things happening again, whether it's to slow down a fast-talking client to confirm exactly what they need, or to spend longer on the project planning to avoid going back to square one further down the line.

DITCH MANUAL PROCESSES

High performers are always open to productive shortcuts.

There are many tools, processes and systems available that can save time and money, while ensuring high-quality results. This is especially the case when tasks need completing manually so be on the lookout for ways you could automate and simplify them.

- When you need to do a lot of writing, try voice recognition software so that you can just dictate rather than spending hours typing into your laptop.
- When you need to work with lists of numbers, transfer them into an Excel spreadsheet so that the data can be easily and accurately manipulated.
- When you need to schedule lots of events, such as multiple one-on-one meetings, use a scheduling app (such as Calendly.com or Youcanbook.me) and then simply share access to your schedule with those you need to meet with.
- When you have recurring pieces of work, always save, replicate and copy any helpful frameworks and templates. This might be as simple as re-using a PowerPoint template for a repeating client presentation format.
- When you need to manually enter data, such as name cards, client orders or business expenses, use scanning tools that takes printouts of receipts or invoices and can upload the key data into a software system.

You're spoiled for choice in terms of automation tools now, so never spend hours doing something manually when simple use of a tool could save you time and eliminate mistakes.

Chapter 46

Go back to basics

You probably use the Microsoft Office suite of tools (or something similar) on a daily basis – typically Word, Outlook, Note or Excel – but are you getting the most out of them? There are many little hacks that can save you time and effort such as:

- In Word, you can edit and re-save pdf files.
- In all Office solutions, you can save time using keyboard shortcuts, such as pressing Ctrl + C to copy, Ctrl + V to paste, and Ctrl + X to cut.
- In Excel, you can insert live data from the internet.
- In all Microsoft Office products, you can enter words or phrases into the search box titled 'tell me' and the relevant command can be instantly performed for you.

Automation can be a lot of small solutions

These few little productivity hacks can help reduce manual data entry and typing, but of course there are many more – too many to list here, so go out and find what would make your life simpler. If it's a chore for you, chances are it was for someone else too and some clever person will have created a workaround. For example:

- With the appropriate web browser settings, you can have your laptop auto fill your personal details into sign-up and application forms.
- You can create email reply templates for when you want to send similar email responses to a large number of people.

REDUCE TIME SPENT IN MEETINGS

Keep meetings short, sweet and simple.

On average we spend 20 per cent of our working time in meetings, according to a survey by Accountemps. Spending a fifth of your time in meetings might be ok if they were all really well run, productive and useful, but evidence suggests otherwise. Doodle, the meeting scheduling app, interviewed over 6,500 customers and concluded that each of us spends two hours a week in useless meetings. Each year this adds up to 13 days wasted.

To increase your productivity, place a higher value on your time and follow a few simple rules:

- Keep meetings short. If something can be achieved in 30 minutes, why schedule an hour-long meeting?
- Be ruthless in ensuring that a clear agenda is created and adhered to.
- Don't allow meetings to overrun because of small talk and discussions wandering off topic.

It's also important to remember that when a meeting cannot be kept short, attendees will lose concentration and become distracted. To counter this, build in regular breaks. The importance of comfort breaks is confirmed by research, with a University of Illinois at Urbana-Champaign study in 2011 concluding that they provide a temporary diversion enabling attendees to regain their focus and attention.

Keep meetings short

Limit your meetings to 30 or 50 minutes in length. Short meetings will help focus the attention of those attending and reduce the sense that people are wasting time by being there:

- Try holding 30-minute meetings with everyone standing rather than sitting. This helps keep discussions short since no one really wants to have to stand up for more than half an hour. These are very common in manufacturing plants and are really effective for daily check-ins with a team or to quickly discuss a single issue.
- Limiting other meetings to 50 minutes and starting them on the hour gives everyone a free 10 minutes and time for a break before starting their next activity.

Be organized

Make sure attendees don't waste time by arriving unprepared, and that there is no time wasting during the meeting itself:

- When inviting colleagues, set clear expectations by giving them a written agenda with timings for each of the agenda items.
- Ask attendees to complete any required pre-reading, and to prepare before-hand anything they'll need to present during the meeting.
- At the start of any meeting nominate someone to be the timekeeper and ask that they keep track of time, warning you all when too much time is being spent on an agenda item. This helps ensure that your meetings always finish on time.
- If meetings exceed 50 minutes in length plan for a short break of 5 or 10 minutes to enable participants to regain their energy and focus.

DON'T BURN YOURSELF OUT

Slow and steady wins the day.

Hard-working people sometimes burn out, and there's a risk that by pushing yourself to achieve more you'll burn out from high levels of stress, exhaustion and overload.

A 2018 Gallup survey found that the impacts of burnout included a rise in people taking sick days, having less confidence in their own work performance and also being more likely to resign from the job. The same survey found that the top five reasons for burnout are:

- unfair treatment at work
- unmanageable workload
- lack of role clarity
- lack of communication and support from their manager
- unreasonable time pressure.

These all link to productivity, particularly the points about an unmanageable workload, time pressures and lack of role clarity. To be productive, you have to learn to work smart and pace yourself. Performing well today is of little value if you're over-worked, drained, and forced to spend the next week recovering.

The secret to your success is to be more of a tortoise than a hare:

- The hare sprints off really quickly, giving him a large lead (and the false perception of being very successful).
- He soon becomes exhausted and needs to rest, only to be overtaken by the tortoise.
- The tortoise is slower but he maintains a constant speed throughout the race, which he goes on to win.

Chapter 48

It's ok to admit you're struggling

Could you sustain your current level of workload without risking burnout? When I ask my coaching clients that question, most say they couldn't.

If your workload, style and pace of working aren't sustainable, have the courage to admit it. Stop pretending that all is ok for fear of appearing weak and incapable. Take action now to avoid overload and exhaustion catching up with you later, at which point your performance and health will suffer.

Find the pace that works for you

Stop and review your working patterns and their impact on you. The easiest way to avoid burning out is to slow down and do less. This can be hard if you have a long to-do list and constant pressure to perform. The secret is for you to continually find ways of working in smarter and more sustainable ways – from saying no and delegating more through to dropping unimportant tasks and automating.

Rest and recover when needed

Obviously there'll be times when you need to over-work, but balance out the intense periods by working at a slower pace when possible and taking breaks. So if you've spent all weekend finalizing an urgent piece of work, have a slow Monday to rest and recover.

ELIMINATE MENTAL OVERLOAD

Busyness is the enemy of productivity.

When you're really busy and overwhelmed, your head will overflow with anxieties about the many different tasks on your plate. You might be worrying about lots of small details, unanswered emails, upcoming meetings, and things people are expecting from you. If you're in this state for too long, you might experience a condition called chronic fatigue and experience symptoms such as:

- forgetfulness
- tiredness
- lack of focus
- mental slowness
- reduced problem-solving ability
- being more prone to distractions
- rigid and less agile thinking.

According to Paul Allen, the creator of a productivity technique called Getting Things Done (GTD), when you feel like this, your productivity can fall as you struggle to focus on your current tasks while your mind is thinking about lots of other things. Allen refers to this as being caught up in open loops of thinking about your obligations at the expense of focusing on what you are actually doing now, creating a situation where:

- your head has no space to focus on what you need to do
- you waste time thinking rather than doing
- you work on tasks without your full focus and attention.

To avoid this productivity drain, empty the mental noise or clutter in your head by using systems which will free you up from obsessing over a long list of tasks that need dealing with.

Chapter 49

Map out what's in your head

Work through the three-part framework summarized below. It's designed to help you process anxieties about your workload, while helping you answer the question 'What should I be focusing on today (or this week)?'.

This simple framework is designed to help you clear your head of work-related worries, and builds on Allen's GTD model as well as on the ideas of creating to-do lists and of judging what is urgent and important to do (covered in Chapter 2 and Chapter 6 respectively).

1 **Collect**: At the start of the day or week, write down every task that crosses your mind. Make sure to capture all of your worries, concerns and thoughts about pending work. Note them all, no matter how small and trivial, in your journal or on your smartphone. You're literally getting all your work worries out of your head and onto paper. Some people do this all the time, even keeping a notebook by their bed to write down what is keeping them awake at night.

2 **Process**: Go through your list deciding how each task needs to be dealt with. Determine what you can ignore, what needs your attention now or later and what might require different attention (for example, you might need to clarify who's really responsible for an unfinished task that has been on your mind).

3 **Map out what you need to do:**

a Delegate and pass to the right people those tasks that are their responsibility and not yours.

b Make a separate note of those tasks that you can ignore and that you've no need to focus on or worry about.

c Update your to-do list so that it only contains tasks that are your responsibility. Make a note by each task of when you need to start working on it and what the deadline is for its completion.

Once you've completed this process and emptied your head of work worries, focus on the one task that you need to do now.

BE PRODUCTIVE WITH YOUR FREE TIME

Weekends and holidays are a chance to be productive in totally different ways.

Being productive shouldn't stop the minute you leave the office or close your laptop. You also want to be smart about how you use your free time, making sure you spend it productively on the non-work-related aspects of your life, whether it's yourself, your health, hobbies, education, family, friends or community.

Protect this free time by not taking your work home with you at weekends, in the evenings and on vacation. For one thing it's also not healthy. One piece of UK 2019 research, published in the *Journal of Epidemiology and Community Health*, found that working in your free time at weekends is linked to increased symptoms of depression, while a University of Sheffield study, also from 2019, concluded that those who work at weekends reported significantly lower levels of happiness than those who do not.

For the purposes of this book though, it's also unproductive: since your mind knows you've got more time to work on tasks, you're unlikely to work as smart, quickly and efficiently as someone who makes sure they finish everything by 5pm on a Friday evening and doesn't reopen their laptop again until Monday morning.

As well as leaving your work at the office and having a great life, the secret to your success is to be productive in all areas including in your free time, and yes, that means applying many of this book's tools and advice to your weekends and family life, including to-do lists, prioritizing activities, taking breaks and having 'me time'.

Plan and prioritize your free time

Create, and keep updated, a non-work-related to-do list which might include activities such as:

- unplanned down time
- time by yourself
- time doing nothing
- time with family
- time with friends

- helping someone do something
- travelling
- exercising
- learning and studying
- resting and recuperating.

It doesn't have to be a detailed to-do list like the one you might create for your day job, but it should capture all the activities that are important to you.

Once you've created a list, prioritize activities and set some timeframes for how you want to spend the upcoming weekend or vacation time. Your challenge is to balance your own needs and wants with the competing demands of your family members. You may need to negotiate and compromise, taking care not to lose the time you need for yourself.

Take your holidays

Not using all of your holiday entitlement each year is nothing to be proud of. It's simply a sign that you're allowing your work and career to consume you.

Always take your full paid holiday allowance even when it's a struggle because of workload. If you cannot take a straight fortnight off work, try taking a couple of days every month to give you a lot of long weekends.

Maximize your weekends

You may have no choice but to work at weekends, particularly if you're working in the retail and hospitality sectors, or perhaps if your job is spread over seven days of the week or you're holding down two or three different jobs to make ends meet. You may feel you've no free time at all or just want to sleep when not working. Do your best to have days off, free evenings and holidays, and use non-work time as productively as you do work time.

REPEAT YOUR SUCCESSES

If it works, do it again.

Repetitive or recurring tasks take up at least 35 per cent of our time, according to the American tech company Asana in their *Anatomy of Work Index* survey report. If much of our daily work keeps repeating itself, why aren't we all experts at our jobs? There are a few possible reasons:

- We're often too busy to think about how we previously completed a similar or identical task.
- Sometimes we don't even realize that a task today mirrors one we completed last month.
- We rarely reflect on what worked well last time around.

We are wasting time and energy if we don't learn the lessons from work we've done before. Take the time to notice when tasks or work processes are repetitive or recurring and use the insights from past mistakes and what worked well to grow and improve your performance.

Chapter 51

Know what tasks will be repeated

Note which of your tasks are either regularly recurring, sometimes need repeating or are one-off and bespoke. Sometimes it may only be parts of tasks that are the same, such as a process to follow.

Systematically replicate success

Here are some techniques that you can experiment with to help you learn from your past work. See which ones work for you:

- **'Lessons learned' reviews**: after completing any task, sit down alone (or with those who helped you do the work) to review and write down what went well and where you may have struggled.
- **Create a cheat sheet**: for tasks that are hard to do really well and based on your lessons learned reviews, create a list of do's and don'ts you can refer to when undertaking the same (or related) tasks in the future.
- **Process manual and instruction guides**: when you find yourself repeating tasks on a regular basis, consider creating a 'how to' guide (if one doesn't already exist). This document can be regularly updated as you discover additional ways to successfully complete the piece of work.
- **Record your work**: record by video or audio a task as you are working on it, in which you might verbally share what you're doing. Recordings can be an easy way to remind you how you completed the tasks.
- **Use service level agreements (SLAs)**: these are agreements that list the agreed deliverables and outputs of a particular process or task. Whenever a task is repeated an SLA provides a helpful guide of what quality of work and deliverables are expected (by your colleagues or the clients you are completing the task for).
- **Templates and pre-settings**: with work that will be duplicated, there may be templates or pre-settings in a system or software program that can be saved and used every time that same task is repeated.

STEP OUT OF YOUR COMFORT ZONE

Don't be afraid of what might go wrong – think of what might go right.

To grow and thrive, you have to be willing to make changes, experiment and do things differently. You have to leave your comfort zone.

A comfort zone is a mental state in which things are familiar and where you feel in control, free of stress and at ease. Examples might be staying in the same job for years, completing your work in the same way every day, living in the same house all your adult life or always driving the same brand of car.

If you're performing really well in your job and have no desire to change, you're very fortunate, but if you do need to improve your performance, then you'll need to step out of your comfort zone.

- If you need to boost your sales, you may need to stop relying on your existing customer base and instead find and connect with new customers.
- If your current product development process is taking too long and you need to shorten it, then you may need to re-engineer and learn new systems and processes.
- If you realize that your quiet and introverted personality is holding you back, you may have to find other ways to show your value and win a promotion.

Being consistently productive means breaking free of comfort zones wherever possible. Given that it's not always obvious when you're stuck in one, that requires a high degree of self-analysis for one thing but as a general mindset, it's about always being willing to adopt new approaches to boost productivity, from learning a new software language, to moving to a new supply chain process through to mastering a new soft skill such as being more persistent or empathic.

Chapter 52

Accept change

Accept that changes are always happening in all aspects of your life. Take a moment to think about all the changes you've observed and experienced in your life and career.

You can fight them, become upset with them, or you can get into the habit of embracing change. In your working life you'll face numerous changes such as revised reporting lines, new job opportunities, updated ways of working, new colleagues joining your team and upgraded systems. No matter whether a change is small and easy or large and challenging, try to understand why it's happening, how you can adapt to it and successfully work with it. By getting into the habit of accepting and flowing with changes, you're allowing your comfort zone to continuously expand.

Kill your darlings

The term 'kill your darlings' refers to stopping doing the things you really enjoy because they no longer serve you. They might have helped you in the past but not any longer. To give an example, you may love being known as the team expert on a particular process with skills so legendary you often take on other people's work for them. Giving up that position and turning the tables – delegating parts of the process to other people – can be painful but may be the only way to boost your productivity.

Be ready for some discomfort

Adopting a new habit or process can be disruptive and might in the short term even lower your level of work performance. This is normal. Persist, and keep the bigger picture in mind. Before long you'll be feeling the benefits.

GET OUT OF YOUR OWN WAY

Silence your inner critic.

Self-defeating and critical thoughts can make you your own worst enemy when it comes to wanting to be more productive. For some of us this is simply the odd moment of doubt about how well we can adapt to something new, but for others, negative thinking can be self-sabotaging and crippling, with their so-called inner critic questioning everything they want to do:

- 'I won't make the deadline, so there's no point in attempting to finish on time.'
- 'I'm not good enough to lead the project team, so it's ok that I'll never be promoted to the project manager role.'
- 'I'm always late for our team meetings, so it's ok if I'm never asked to chair our department discussions.'
- 'I don't deserve to be the first to finish, so I may as well not bother trying.'
- 'I'll never have the courage to say "no", so I may as well accept that I'll always be an over-worked people pleaser.'

It doesn't matter how well you master the advice in this book if your inner critic is always waiting in the wings to sabotage you. Constantly listening to an inner voice telling you you're not good enough saps your energy and your productivity, but you can learn to control it and become less impacted by it.

Take control

Teach yourself not to over-react to every thought and worry that enters your mind, particularly when you're doing a new or difficult task and your mind is telling you about everything that could possibly go wrong.

- Find ways to become calmer by practising regular meditation, breathing exercises, yoga or any other type of calming activities. A calmer mind is less likely to over-react to anxious thoughts and worries that suddenly appear in your head.
- Understand that these random and critical thoughts are not *you* – and you can talk back to them by silently saying, 'Thanks for sharing your worries with me but you can go away now. I'm ok and am quite capable of achieving my goal.'
- Seek the support of trusted colleagues, close friends or family by opening up to them about how you sometimes self-sabotage, asking them to be ready to give you helpful and positive words of encouragement whenever you need help countering negative self-talk.

Your critical and self-defeating thoughts might have been with you since childhood and their causes could be intertwined with your personality traits and your self-esteem. As a result, eliminating them might require professional help from a therapist, and ideally one who is expert in cognitive behavioural therapy (CBT). CBT is based on the idea that changing your negative thinking and habits improves your life and work performance.

CREATE THE IDEAL PHYSICAL ENVIRONMENT

Find your happy place.

We're all creatures of comfort. Just like anyone else, you're going to struggle to be productive if you're distracted by environmental factors, such as being too hot or surrounded by too much pollution, noise or vibrations. Research confirms the importance of your environment for productivity:

- In a paper published by the US Department of Energy Office of Scientific and Technical Information, researchers found that a person's productivity is impacted by the temperature of their workplace.
- A 2019 survey of 2,000 people across the UK, US and Australia conducted by the flooring company Interface and Radius Global Market Research found that 69 per cent of the respondents said that noise levels at workplaces had a detrimental impact on their levels of productivity, creativity and concentration.
- In 2017 research, summarized in the *Harvard Business Review*, US academic researchers found that better air quality correlates with improved decision-making performance.
- A City University London paper looking at various pieces of research concluded that there's a strong association between the quality of lighting in a work location and the performance of those working there.

So how do you create the ideal work environment for productivity?

Find what works for you and your colleagues

Everyone is unique and what may seem like a comfortable temperature to you might seem chilly to others. The secret is to find the right balance that works for you and everyone you share your work area with.

Focus on the key elements:

- **Air flow**: avoid a stuffy room with a lack of fresh air. As you spend more time in it, the air will become stale and the oxygen level will fall, making you sleepy and less sharp. You might want to experiment with a small fan by your work station or to leave a window partially open.
- **Lighting**: consider if you need to invest in better lighting, perhaps replacing some uncomfortable white lightbulbs with some warmer yellow ones.
- **Noise**: if you're living in a noisy environment, maybe it's time to ask others to be quieter, turn down the radio in the office or keep your door closed.
- **Temperature**: are you normally too warm or too cold working at your desk? Perhaps you need to work with a fan or air conditioner during the summer months and ensure that the heating system during winter isn't set so high that you become too hot and stuffy.

Relocate if needed

If you're in a position to choose where you work from, and you struggle to work well in your current work environment, consider moving to a better work setting.

- If you're working at home, consider switching your home office to another room in your house.
- In the office, seek out an empty work area that provides you with more natural light or is quieter.

IDENTIFY YOUR LEAKS

Look after the minutes, and the hours will take care of themselves.

No matter how efficient you think you are, if you don't plug any small un-productive gaps, you'll never optimize your performance. It's like having a car tyre with air slowly escaping through small punctures that you haven't been able to locate and repair. Little wasteful moments can easily pass under your radar, but together they can slowly drain your time and energy. For example, think of the time lost when you:

- lie in bed, after your alarm has gone off, worrying about work issues
- read every email in detail, even when you know they're not important
- constantly switch between tasks and need time to reacquaint yourself with each task where you'd previously left off
- are always 5–10 minutes early for meetings and sit doing nothing, when you could have been finishing an important email
- break off from work every few minutes to check your social media
- allow your mind to wander in meetings.

None of these time drains is particularly devastating in isolation, but they don't tend to exist in isolation. You need to address all of your productivity leaks to be at your most efficient, taking time to discover what they are and how to plug them.

Chapter **55**

Identify the leaks

Productivity leaks compound over time so try to resist the temptation to dismiss them as trivial and too small to worry about. Small things happening on a regular basis can easily turn into a large issue. Ten minutes a day equates to over 40 hours a year which is the equivalent of one lost working week.

Over a couple of weeks, observe how you spend your time and take a note of those small behaviours that might qualify as productivity leaks. For each potentially unproductive habit decide if you should:

* eliminate it because it's clearly wasting your time and energy, or
* continue with it because it might be a beneficial coping habit. It might be a moment to de-stress and step back from your workload. Coping habits can have a positive impact on your overall productivity.

Overcome wasteful habits

Deciding how you'll overcome wasteful habits depends on what they are. You'll find advice throughout the book for the most common culprits.

Don't blame yourself

Don't beat yourself up about productivity leaks. It's only human to lose a few minutes here and there thinking or doing things that may not be helpful to you or your work. The important thing is that today you've committed to action.

MASTER HYBRID WORKING

You can be productive wherever you're working from.

The global COVID-19 pandemic forced many of us to work from home for extended periods of time, and the new norm is to divide the working week between your office and home working. We tend to perform better when we feel motivated by our work environment, and fortunately the majority of people enjoy hybrid working:

- A 2021 global survey by Accenture of over 9,000 people found that 83 per cent prefer hybrid working, particularly when they can work from home at least 25 per cent of the time.
- 77 per cent of UK respondents in a 2021 global survey by the recruitment group Adecco also said they like mixing working from home with being in the office.

Combining working from home with being in your office brings a range of pros and cons:

Possible pros of hybrid working	Possible cons of hybrid working
Opportunity to work quietly at home, without colleagues around you	Family interruptions
Can plan face-to-face work for when in the office, and save work you can do on your own for when you're home working	Needing to take your office things back and forth between home and office
Less time spent commuting to the office each week	Emerging trend of having to 'hot desk', and not having your own permanent workspace
When at home, more freedom to plan how you work and how the day is used	Harder to plan face-to-face work if staff not in office on the same days

The secret to your success is to optimize the pros while ensuring that the cons don't negatively impact your productivity.

Optimize the positives

When working at home you can decide how you'll be productive without needing to appear busy and always sitting at your desk. No one can see you and you can use this freedom in a positive way by experimenting and finding ways of working that really suit your personality, motivations and energy levels.

This might mean you work intensively for a couple of hours before breaking to take a short walk or to visit the gym before returning to your desk.

Alternatively, you might prefer to start work at 6am and finish in the evening with a long break in the middle of the day.

You can also decide which tasks are better suited to being at home and which are better in the more collaborative office environment. To ensure that your time in the office is as productive as possible, why not agree with your colleagues to co-ordinate particular days of the week when you'll all be together and schedule meetings or group activities that would benefit from being face to face on those days?

Minimize the negatives

Try to make working from home as efficient and productive as being in the office, and explore the following:

- Set some boundaries with those you live with about when you need to be left alone to focus. This might entail locking yourself away and letting your family know when you can and cannot be disturbed.
- If you're having internet connection issues, explore upgrading your internet speed and bandwidth.
- Use the opportunity of working alone to plan your day in a way that works for you.
- If you struggle to be productive at home, your boss will probably appreciate your honesty and be delighted to have you in the office more frequently than your company's policy requires.

SEEK A MENTOR

It's easier to walk in someone else's footsteps.

A mentor can elevate your performance to the next level by helping you master all kinds of productive ways of working. People often get confused about the difference between mentoring and coaching, so let's go with the European Mentoring and Coaching Council's definition of mentoring as 'a learning relationship, involving the sharing of skills, knowledge, and expertise between a mentor and mentee through developmental conversations, experience sharing, and role modelling. The relationship may cover a wide variety of contexts and is an inclusive two-way partnership for mutual learning that values differences.'

Mentoring has become more widespread in recent years, and many well-known and successful people have spoken about their own mentors:

- Bill Gates has shared about the importance of the mentoring advice he has received from Warren Buffett.
- Sir Richard Branson once said that the mentoring (related to the airline sector) he received from Sir Freddie Laker was invaluable.

Best-practice mentoring consists of conversations between you and your mentor, during which the two of you can talk and explore in confidence any topic and issue which can help you to learn and grow. From a productivity perspective, you would typically want a mentor to help you become expert in tackling any performance-related issues and challenges you face today, such as:

- learning how to prioritize tasks
- becoming better at time management
- pushing back and saying 'no'
- maintaining your focus and energy
- dealing with overload
- avoiding distractions
- making meetings optimal
- overcoming email overload.

Chapter 57

Decide what help you need

Before approaching potential mentors, you need to know what you want to learn and explore with a mentor. Sense check this with any feedback that you've recently received from your boss, team members, colleagues and other stakeholders through performance reviews or 360-degree feedback. Share with your colleagues your plan to work with a mentor and ask them what particular issues and challenges they suggest you should focus on.

Find ideal mentors

- Find a formal mentor who is not your boss, since they might be too close to you to be able to offer you independent and objective advice and support. This is particularly true if you want mentoring advice about how to work with your boss!
- Think about asking one of your senior colleagues who has had similar work experiences to you, someone who has successfully done what you aspire to do.
- Choosing a mentor in your company is good because they'll understand your working culture, contexts, environment and players but you might benefit from the different perspective of a mentor from another organization or sector.
- Consider asking colleagues who may be peers at your level, or may even be more junior than you, if you feel they have particular experiences or skills that you'd like to learn more about.

TRUST OTHERS

Trust is the glue that holds us all together.

In today's working world, none of us is alone and we all depend on other people to enable our success. This can take many different forms:

- You need someone to review and check your work.
- You need other people to provide you with input, data or answers.
- You co-create solutions and outputs with colleagues in a project team.
- You rely upon a key supplier to sell you components.
- You lead a team and you must continually work together.

The key success factor in all of these interactions is trust. To be at your most productive you need to be able to trust everyone you work with on every level including their promises, assumptions, statements, goals, quality of work and decisions.

When you're working in an environment without trust, it generates additional work for you because you may feel compelled to:

- double check other people's work
- seek a second or even third opinion
- take on work you would otherwise delegate
- undertake any number of other actions which only increases your own workload.

When trust is lacking, relationships often deteriorate because the other person senses your lack of trust. This can create friction, make them upset and reticent to help you. The net result is that you have more to do yourself and your productivity takes a hit.

Chapter **58**

Carry out a trust audit

On a regular basis ask yourself two questions:

1 How much do I trust everybody around me, and how can I maximize these levels of trust?
2 Is there anyone who may not fully trust me – and if so, how can I resolve it?

It's quite easy to think about who you trust and who you've got doubts about. It might be a little more challenging to consider who may not fully trust you, particularly given the normal human tendency to think we are completely trustworthy.

With those you suspect of not trusting you, try to have an open and frank discussion to hear their feelings about working with you and any concerns they may have. Feel free to express your wish to earn and maintain their trust.

Recognize your own patterns

Review the level of trust you have in other people. Make sure it's accurate and not based on bias or poor information:

- You may have unconscious biases which need addressing, such as more easily trusting men than women, or more readily believing what older colleagues tell you compared to younger ones.
- Explore if you're unfairly holding something against a colleague because of a one-off mistake they made in the past. It might be time to let go and re-set the relationship.
- Question whether you tend to trust too easily based on positive personality traits. Just because someone is friendly doesn't make them great at their job. You might need to learn to be more balanced and objective in how you form opinions about people.

MASTER YOUR MEMORY

Your memory is a muscle – remember to exercise it.

Unless you've got a photographic memory, there's a limit to what you can memorize. We've all had those moments of forgetting it's a friend's birthday or where we parked the car. But what if you forget something that has a negative impact on your work performance, such as:

- the content for an important presentation you are giving in 20 minutes' time
- a submission deadline that makes you liable for penalty fines
- what a client requested or what was agreed in a departmental meeting?

It's natural to forget things when you're relying solely on your own memory. Repeated studies have confirmed the validity of what is called the 'forgetting curve', which was discovered a century ago by Hermann Ebbinghaus. It shows that without any retention tools or systems, we quickly forget what we've just learned or been told, and on average we forget:

- 50 per cent after an hour
- 70 per cent after one day
- 90 per cent after a week.

In addition, by trying to remember information we use brain capacity that could be better used for more important activities. This was confirmed by University of Münster research published in the journal *Ergonomics*, which found that people's decision-making was improved (and they were less stressed) when they had online access to information compared to having to memorize it and recall the same things themselves without any external help.

You will increase your productivity if you accept how easy it is to forget things and, instead of relying on your own memory, use other methods and tools to help you recall key facts, dates and information.

Write it down

Get into the habit of recording on paper or online everything that needs remembering and later recalling:

- During or immediately after a meeting write down important decisions, notes, actions and points of agreement. This can later be shared as a meeting minute or post-meeting action plan.
- With online meetings on platforms such as Zoom, Webex and Microsoft Teams, it's possible, with the participants' consent, to record the meetings so they can be listened to later.
- After an important phone call or discussion, follow up with an email which summarizes what has been agreed.
- Use your smartphone as a voice recorder to record voice memos.
- When you meet new people make a note of their names and key details about them, so that when you meet again you don't make an embarrassing mistake.
- Take photos or screenshots of things that you'd like to be able to refer back to and review later.

Double check things

To help you later remember what you hear today, practise the skills of being an active listener which were explored in Chapter 38, including clarifying and summarizing what someone has said.

Improve your memory

There'll always be moments when you're unable to record everything that's being shared with you or you have no access to past meeting minutes, a confirmation email or a colleague to ask. To recall what was discussed, you'll have to rely upon your own memory. Keep your mind sharp with mental exercises and activities. Working out your brain really is like working any other muscle. Keep it in good shape and work it out regularly, particularly as you age.

ALIGN YOUR WORK WITH THE TEAM

Swim with the current – not against it.

When you're working well with colleagues and all of your plans, schedules and decisions are aligned, everything feels easier to achieve, including your goals and objectives.

Creating and maintaining this level of alignment and coordination isn't easy, because so often people work in disconnected ways, either by accident or intentionally. Here are some examples you might recognize:

- You create a detailed budget for a product launch, only to learn that your finance colleague has spent hours creating a similar forecast. You've both wasted your valuable time and failed to come together to produce an aligned forecast.
- You plan an important project review meeting, but half the team miss it because your colleague called a departmental team meeting at exactly the same time.
- You plan to visit a couple of key clients, only to discover that your marketing colleague has just done the same thing. You both missed the opportunity to visit them together and you know that it doesn't look good if you visit them so soon after your colleague.

Poor alignment and coordination are normally the result of poor communication, but they're also caused by people working in their own silos and not caring about what anyone else is doing. As well as wasting time, money and energy, this is sub-optimal because you fail to create positive synergies together. It's demotivating and resulting disagreements can turn into open conflicts. In such an environment it's impossible to remain productive.

Chapter 60

Be open and share

Meet regularly. Have catch-up meetings with colleagues to share what each of you is working on and planning to do in the next few weeks. Be open to finding synergies in terms of how you might help each other, and be honest about where you may have competing interests or demands, and where disagreements and conflict may arise.

Align your diaries – openly share your own schedule and make an effort to check other people's calendars when inviting them to important meetings, to avoid creating conflicting events. In addition to internal meetings, coordinate dates and times of key events, for example liaising with a colleague on external visits to clients or suppliers.

Synchronize your to-do lists and action plans – share them with any colleagues your work overlaps with or where one of you depends on the other. Use your common sense to decide what aspects of each other's work needs aligning – either in terms of goals or key performance indicators, tasks, deliverables and workload, or in the use of shared resources.

Be mindful of internal politics

There will be times when a colleague may not be willing to help you – either because they're too busy or because they're jealous or threatened by your success. Sadly, too many people are happy to see others struggle or even fail. To remain productive, you'll need to decide how to optimally respond in these types of situations.

- You could remain silent and simply do the work yourself or find others to help you.
- You might reduce your future reliance by changing how you do things.
- If you're unable to perform well without the help and support of your reluctant colleague, you may need to escalate this issue to your bosses.

STAND UP WHEN WORKING

We all need to stand up more.

The UK's British Heart Foundation estimates that on average we sit for at least 9.5 hours per day, with the number rising if you have a desk job and commute to and from work.

There are well-researched benefits to standing while working. In 2016 research published in the journal *IIE Transactions on Occupational Ergonomics and Human Factors*, a group of call centre workers were given standing desks and their productivity rose by at least 45 per cent. A similar conclusion was reached in a 2018 *British Medical Journal* study of NHS workers who were allowed to stand while working at raised desks. In both studies people were less tired, happier and their work performance improved compared to colleagues sitting at normal height desks. Standing can also improve other aspects of your health, with one 2016 study in the *Journal of Physical Activity and Health* showing that we burn more calories when standing compared to sitting.

There are also productivity benefits to holding meetings and one-on-one discussions while standing (or even walking):

- Standing meetings tend to be much more effective compared to having everyone sit around a table together. When everyone is standing in a huddle or circle, the meeting tends to be quicker and more efficient, with everyone more focused since they are not as easily distracted by their PC, paperwork or phone.
- Standing meetings also improve the quality of discussion and brainstorming, with one 2014 US study published in the journal *Social Psychological and Personality Science* finding that people who stand are more likely to open up and share their ideas.
- The same applies whether the meeting involves a group or a one-on-one standing or walking catch-up with a colleague.

Chapter 61

No more sitting

Look out for opportunities to stand in your day-to-day-life:

- Ditch your normal height desk and use an adjustable height one so that you can regularly stand to do your work.
- When you're commuting to work, try to stand.
- When you're standing, be upright. Avoid slouching or leaning your neck forward. It helps if you raise your phone, tablet, newspaper or book to your head height rather than holding them lower.
- It would be hard to stand all day. Take short breaks and wear comfortable shoes to ease the pressure on your feet.

Walk, talk and think

Walking helps you stay physically fit and it also helps keep your mind fresh and alert. When you want to think through something, go for a walk, even if it's just around your office or home.

Try taking phone calls while walking – wear an earphone and carry a notebook to capture key points.

Use your smartphone or watch to measure how many steps you walk each day, and set yourself daily targets.

Stand and meet

Conduct your meetings while standing, unless they're very long ones. In those situations you might rotate sessions between sitting and standing.

During online meetings stand up with your laptop or screen raised to your head height. Try attending them on your phone so that you walk while listening and speaking.

If you're used to the agile/scrum ways of working, you may already be used to having daily standing meetings. If not, it might take a few weeks for you and your colleagues to become used to standing.

KNOW WHY YOU'RE DOING WHAT YOU'RE DOING

Always know the 'why' – this will give reason and meaning to your work.

At least a third of us find our work meaningless. A 2015 YouGov survey found that 37 per cent of respondents in the UK said their job achieved nothing meaningful, with only 50 per cent saying the opposite and 13 per cent being unsure. In a World Economic Forum-quoted 2017 survey of 12,000 professionals, half the respondents said their jobs held no significance or meaning for them. In recent years, particularly since the COVID-19 pandemic, these already high percentages are likely to have risen.

What chance do you have of performing well and being productive if you find your job meaningless? It's a lot easier to work hard, excel and invest the focus and effort you need on a task when you know the purpose and meaning behind your work.

Working each day without meaning is boring, demotivating and potentially soul-destroying. Fyodor Dostoevsky observed that to break a person you just needed to give them meaningless work, a tactic that was supposedly used in Soviet gulags where prisoners went crazy being forced to dig and re-fill holes in the ground.

The extent to which a piece of work is likely to be meaningful depends on how well you can visualize what happens to what you've done. This is about being given the full picture so that you can see the part your job role plays within your organization and beyond.

Chapter 62

Find meaning and purpose

Every time you take on a piece of work, think about why it needs completing and what it'll be used for. You might need to be persistent as your senior colleagues probably won't be used to being asked about the value of individual tasks. They might not have the answers but keep pushing. Once you understand how your work fits into the bigger picture, it will become more meaningful for you, making you in turn more focused and productive. If your job involves creating detailed reports for example, you should know why they're needed, who reads them and how they're used.

Make needed changes

Push back and say 'no' if you find you're being repeatedly asked to do work that has no real value to your organization and/or no meaning for you. If no one actually uses the reports you're writing, work with your boss on how your time could be better used. If you can't make your current workload more meaningful it might be time to move on.

Help others find meaning

Make sure everyone you work with also appreciates the value and importance of their work. It's not enough just to pay them well. At some point in all our lives we look for more than monetary reward for our efforts. We need purpose too.

NO MORE OVERTIME

Less is more.

When you think of productive people, you tend to imagine someone who works harder and spends longer at work than most of us do. If you thought this, you'd be wrong. The most productive people know that the longer you spend working, the less productive you become.

According to 2014 research from Stanford University's Professor John Pencavel, the magic number of hours to work each week is 50 – and beyond that your productivity per hour falls sharply. He found that when you exceed 55 hours per week, extra hours worked yield zero extra performance. In other words you'd be wasting your time, as well as probably falling asleep on the job!

This idea that working less is more productive is confirmed by various pieces of research:

- A 2015 *Harvard Business Review* published study by Erin Reid found that line managers could not see any difference in the amount of work completed by staff who worked 80 hours per week compared to those who only pretended to work as long.
- In Japanese research published in 2021 by Shangguan et al., researchers concluded that working fewer hours increased a person's productivity, in part because they would be less tired and would make fewer mistakes.

The message is clear: focus on working well for a maximum of 50 hours per week, and don't fool yourself into thinking that working longer will improve your performance.

Stay within your agreed working hours

Set yourself a goal of only working in line with your company's policies and your employment contract. This is not because you're stubbornly working to rule but to ensure that you stay under the magic 50 hours per week, avoiding productivity decline.

Expected working hours vary by country, but are typically seven to eight hours per day. On this basis, in a typical week you might work 40 hours at the office. Once you've added a few extra hours for checking emails at home and occasionally staying an hour or two longer in the office, you'll be close to 50, but this should be the absolute maximum.

If all goes well, you'll soon be working smart enough to avoid those extra hours, and you might even be in a position to move to a four- or three-day working week!

When you do need to work longer than normal, try to rest and recover by taking a day or half day off in lieu. If you don't take these recovery times, you're likely to become drained and eventually burn out, as we've already seen.

Never support others to over-work

If you rely on others to help you complete your own work, there's little point you working reasonable hours while they're left to work 60–80 hours a week. At some point, their long hours will impact the quality of their work as well as their levels of motivation. Help and encourage them to work smarter, to work their agreed hours and avoid continual overtime.

PLANT SEEDS

Plant the acorn today that will become the oak tree of tomorrow.

Performing well *today* is often the result of groundwork you laid months or even years ago. To maximize your productivity in the future you need to invest your time and effort in things that won't necessarily give you instant results but which will lay the foundations for future success. It's about making choices today that may bring no short-term benefit but have the potential to be very productive in the long term. This can take many forms:

- investing money and time in learning a new skill
- developing a working relationship with a client who might only be able to buy from you two years down the line because they have 24 months remaining on a fixed-term contract
- hiring an inexperienced college leaver hoping they'll grow into a successful team member
- making the time for therapy or coaching today to hone your productivity in the years ahead.

The secret is to be willing to invest your time and energy now, knowing that the return on investment – in terms of improved performance or productivity – isn't guaranteed and will only come in the future.

Plant as many seeds as possible

Think like a gardener. What 'trees' do you want to have in the future? These are your goals and aspirations in terms of work performance and achievements, and the skills you need to master. Your metaphorical trees will be unique to you and might include things as varied as:

- become a qualified accountant and tax expert
- be able to run a small business
- learn to speak French and use it in your work
- be promoted into your boss's job
- be an expert day trader
- become an accredited life coach
- be a recognized chef
- only work four days a week.

Now work backwards and decide what you need to do today to ensure that in one, five or ten years' time you'll have achieved these objectives. Make a detailed plan of action and set aside the money, energy and time to start working on your plan.

Don't be knocked off course

Avoid the natural tendency to focus on activities that'll bring you more immediate reward or that seem more urgent or important compared to tasks that will only yield results in the medium to longer term. Make time for both. Remember that it's better to be over-stretched today than to look back later and regret things you didn't do.

IF IN DOUBT, COMMUNICATE

Sharpen your communication skills to work smarter.

In today's interconnected world, you cannot succeed alone. Being an effective communicator is essential. You can complete some of your tasks alone in silence, but at some point, you'll need input, support, advice and help from other people. It stands to reason that communications skills are widely ranked as a key career success factor:

• In a survey by Chartered Accountants Australia and New Zealand, communication skills were ranked by employers as the most important skill of the future.
• The website Careersinstem.com analysed four similar surveys and arrived at the same conclusion – that communication skills are the top employability skill needed in today's workplace.

These results should be no surprise because it's only through communication that you're able to express essential qualities such as direction, instruction, empathy, respect, feeling valued, appreciation, agreement, trust and friendliness. Qualities that motivate other people to support you in your work.

We all have room for improvement. Even more experienced colleagues who've risen to become leaders struggle. A US Harris Poll summarized in the *Harvard Business Review* found that 69 per cent of managers are not comfortable when communicating with their teams.

Strengthening your communication skills is a core productivity technique. Aim to become expert in verbal as well as non-verbal forms of communication and learn to select and use the ideal medium of communication for each situation that you face.

It is better to over- than under-communicate

In employee engagement surveys it's common for people to complain about a lack of information sharing. To avoid this complaint being directed at you, always speak up and share. Repeat key messages or instructions, have regular team meetings, one-on-one catch-ups and discussions.

Master your words

To ensure that all of your communication is optimal, master the four inter-connected ways we communicate:

• **Verbally**: while drafting an email, speech or presentation think through what you need to say. Choose words, phrases and arguments that are appropriate. Share your draft wording with a trusted colleague if you want a second opinion, and consider using online editing tools such as Grammarly.com, Prowritingaid.com or Languagetool.org.

• **Non-verbally**: when communicating visually, be sure to control your movements and expressions. Avoid off-putting habits such as putting your hands in front of your face when you speak, swinging your arms or looking away.

• **Para-verbally**: when speaking with others, in person or online, make sure that what you're saying isn't overshadowed by bad habits such as pausing for too long, stuttering, or making too many 'mmm' and 'ahhh' sounds.

• **Appearance**: just as your non-verbal body language should never distract from your message, your physical appearance (including choice of attire) should also support your communication messages.

Choose the right medium

To make your communication as impactful as possible, think carefully about which medium you will use. This will depend on the specific context based on the intended audience and type of message, but will normally include:

• emailing (to one or more people)
• one-on-one in person
• one-on-one on the phone/online
• team meeting or discussion
• large gathering (e.g. town hall)
• writing a letter, memo, blog, newsletter or online post
• drafting a report or paper
• messaging app such as Teams or WhatsApp.

CELEBRATE YOUR SUCCESSES

After the sweat and toil of a difficult task, be sure to pause at the end to raise a glass.

When was the last time you took a moment to celebrate your success? Most of us never do. We jump from one task to the next without pausing to enjoy the moment. What you might not realize is that it's healthy and productive to celebrate your completed tasks.

In a study published in the *Harvard Business Review*, involving 12,000 diary entries from 238 employees in seven companies, researchers found that observing and writing about your successes at work is motivational and that pausing to reflect on positive progress boosts self-confidence, which energizes you to perform even better. So stopping to recognize success increases motivation and confidence.

The most productive people go one step beyond simply recognizing achievements. They celebrate them, either alone or with their team. This is even more motivating and confidence-building and brings a number of additional benefits:

- Celebration is a very public and positive form of recognition that will make you and your colleagues feel very valued and engaged. This in turn has a positive impact on your future performance.
- It gives you permission to pause, re-charge and take a break before moving to the next item on your to-do list.
- It's an opportunity to explore what more can be done and to set even bolder goals. Ask yourself questions such as 'If I've been able to complete this goal today, how much more can I achieve next time?'.

Recognize success

Spot and acknowledge when you've done a good job. What's the point of working hard on something only to ignore the moment when you've completed it? Overcome any tendencies to downplay your achievements or to be too modest and humble about the part you've played. Share the news with relevant people such as your boss, colleagues or clients.

Write about your achievements in your journal or diary, commenting on how it makes you feel, and describe what you did to complete the task including any useful hacks or shortcuts you discovered.

When you're working with other people, it's even more important that you stop to recognize what has been achieved. If you neglect to do so, you risk alienating and de-motivating your colleagues.

Explore ways of celebrating

It's very simple. Every time you achieve something, take a moment to reward yourself and those who worked on the task with you. It doesn't matter what you do, just make sure it's positive, uplifting, feel-good and motivating. Some ideas are:

• ring a bell in the office
• buy cupcakes
• create a team video
• go for a team lunch
• give thank you cards.

Surprise yourself and your team by not doing what everyone expects. If you've always had team lunches as a reward, do something different. Naturally the size of the success will determine the size of celebration. I recently read of a tech company founder who successfully sold her company and gave all of her staff and their families first-class plane tickets and $10,000 spending money.

MASTER DEEP WORKING

Deep work is critical for focus and enhanced productivity.

Nothing beats an extended period of time working on a single task with your full powers of concentration for training your brain for increased productivity. Labelled 'deep work' by the US academic and author Cal Newport, periods of focused work and intense concentration are essential, particularly if you're working on intellectually demanding, complicated tasks. Work like this can't easily be completed in short bursts or with multi-tasking.

Deep working enables you to out-perform those who've never developed the ability to deep dive into anything. It's a useful way to complete challenging, or what psychologists call cognitively demanding, work, such as:

• researching for and writing a book
• solving a really sophisticated and hard to understand problem
• learning how to use a new and detailed system or software language
• quickly mastering a foreign language
• managing a complicated system or organization through a crisis.

Deep work might seem easy: shut the door and focus on one piece of work for as long as needed to complete it. In reality though, it takes quite a lot of systematic intention, discipline and repetition. It can be very mentally tiring.

How and when you practise deep work depends on what kinds of tasks you need to complete. For most people it will be about dividing your working week between periods of deep work and of more normal work which don't require the same attention and focus, but permanent deep work is ideal when your job involves focusing only on very complicated and demanding pieces of work.

In today's increasingly technology-driven world, there will always be moments when deep working is the most productive way of working, no matter what kind of job role you're working in.

Learn how to 'deep work'

Being able to focus and avoid distractions is fundamental to becoming a deep-working expert. Use the following tips to try to maximize your opportunities for deep work:

- Decide when you want to do your deep work. If you're going to work in this way for only part of your working week, choose the days and times when you're most productive and awake, and block those periods in your diary for the next few weeks.
- Set aside appropriate time depending on how much of your work requires you to intensely focus and concentrate. If in one week you blocked too little or too much time, simply adjust the amount of time set aside in the weeks ahead.
- Be clear about what you want to achieve during these periods. When I'm writing, I set aside a few hours to intensively focus on completing one draft chapter. What's your equivalent and are you setting aside enough time to complete it well?
- You may need some processes or rituals to help you focus and concentrate, since your willpower may not be enough. Once you've found somewhere quiet, hide your phone and turn off laptop notifications.
- Balance out periods of deep work with break times. Your mind will need a rest after such intense, focused concentration.

CHANGE WHAT NEEDS CHANGING

If you aren't being productive today, ask yourself: 'What can I change?'

I love the saying that 'if you do what you've always done, you'll get what you've always got'. That doesn't apply to you of course because you're reading this book, so you're clearly open to change.

Facing change isn't easy and most people find it challenging. That's understandable given that any kind of work-related change typically involves dealing with a combination of:

- doing new and different tasks
- facing the unknown
- learning new ways of working
- not being sure of how to do something
- being unclear what happens next
- working with new goals and expectations from others
- mastering new systems and skills
- struggling and failing
- getting unexpected results.

In addition to these challenges, we go through our own internal reactions to change. These occur in five predictable stages, based on the work of the psychiatrist Elisabeth Kübler-Ross and her research into dealing with grief:

1 **Denial**: when faced with the need to improve your productivity you might put it off, ignoring a new productivity app, thinking it won't help you.
2 **Anger**: you might be upset and confused at the idea of adopting a new way of working.
3 **Bargaining**: you might try to push back and negotiate with your boss, asking questions like 'do I really need to start using this new system?'.
4 **Depression**: you're likely to feel demotivated and upset when you really don't like a change, and although you may implement the new process, you're likely to do it very half-heartedly.
5 **Acceptance**: there's always light at the end of the tunnel and stage 5 is one of positively accepting, implementing and working with the change.

These stages are normal and inevitable. The secret to success is to get through the first four negative stages as quickly as possible, leaving you to focus your time and energy on the final stage.

Chapter 68

Embrace change

Recognize when you are experiencing any of the first four stages of change – denial, anger, bargaining or depression. It's natural to feel this way but it's not ok to stay there for long.

- Denial links to procrastination (there were tips on managing that in Chapter 14).
- Overcoming feelings of anger or depression links to developing your emotional intelligence and creating a positive mindset. (For more on that, read my other book, *100 Things Successful People Do*).
- Being stuck in the bargaining stage links to your level of denial, anger and depression. You'll only be willing to stop negotiating and arguing when you're no longer upset or in denial.

Do whatever you can to get in a more positive state of acceptance, where you can say to yourself: 'It's not going to be easy to implement this change, but I get it – it will improve my work processes and be worth the effort.'

You don't have to be 100 per cent behind a new change, but if you need to work with it, then quickly embrace the change anyway. Jump in with both feet even if you're still having some doubts about the merits of the change or concerns about how you'll successfully implement it. By doing so you can be a role model to your colleagues.

ACCEPT WHAT YOU CANNOT CHANGE

Practise acceptance – sometimes things cannot be changed.

Your drive to improve performance by maximizing productivity will often face road blocks and diversions. You can't always take a straight line because situations arise that you cannot change. Take these three hypothetical scenarios:

A You want to install new supply chain software in your department and have it 'go live' in two days' time, but your IT colleague has discovered that the new software isn't compatible with your team's computers.

B You work all week to prepare a presentation for the senior management team, only to be told that the CEO has asked your boss to attend and present instead of you.

C Your client needs a kitchen renovation completed by Christmas and offers you a bonus to finish the work by then, but the brand of units she wants will only be available in the New Year.

Productive people always try to respond to unexpected road blocks and changes in an optimal way, and they never waste their time trying to change something that's 'cast in stone'. They're also particularly mindful of not letting the time and effort they've invested to date blind them to reality. Known as the 'sunk cost bias', this is where you might hold onto something for too long simply because you've invested so much of your time in creating it in the first place.

At some point you have to be ready to let go and accept when something is not going to change. Letting go enables you to re-focus your time and energy on things you can make happen and work productively on.

Chapter 69

Be clear on what you can and cannot change

When is it ok to accept and when do you push back and fight? In the previous examples do you try to change the situation so that the outcomes from your viewpoint are optimal by:

A quickly pushing to get approval to buy software-compatible PCs so that the software can be installed and launched asap?

B contacting the CEO and asking her to change her mind and let you present?

C encouraging your client to accept a different brand of kitchen units that are readily available to be installed by mid-December?

If you're unsuccessful with these requests, do you accept the outcomes because they cannot be changed, or do you keep pushing? This is where you need to be wise and not let stubbornness get the better of you.

Make productive detours

Once you've accepted that something will not change, you need to plan how you'll work around it. This may involve you thinking out of the box to brainstorm the ideal solutions, such as:

A delaying the software launch and in the interim staying with the existing system, or finding an alternative software solution that will work on your office PCs

B positively supporting your boss to understand your presentation and help them edit and present it really well

C accepting you've lost the bonus, and assuring your client that you'll install the new units as soon as possible in the New Year – you could also offer to source some spare appliances so your client is able to cook at home over the festive holiday.

BE PRODUCTIVE AFTER MEETINGS

A meeting without anything put to paper is just a chat!

Your time is limited and you're expected to attend many different meetings during your working week. Building on the effective meetings advice from Chapter 22, it's essential that after any meeting you've attended there is 100 per cent written clarity on what has been agreed and who is responsible for the actions. Without having this you risk:

- wasting your time on the same post-meeting tasks as someone else
- important tasks being completed incorrectly or forgotten about
- accusations between you and your colleagues about who was supposed to have done what.

Ensure that someone writes up the agreed actions in the form of meeting minutes or an action plan. Minutes tend to be more formal than an action plan. Depending on the nature of the meeting there are sometimes legal requirements to create very structured minutes that include details such as the time the meeting started and ended, who the chair was as well as any agreed follow-up actions.

The minutes or action plan can be typed up during the meeting or afterwards. The benefit of doing it during the meeting and screen sharing them is that you can all agree to what is being written, rather than having to wait for an emailed version to be sent to you.

Make an action plan

Follow these tips for meeting minutes or action plans:

- Make sure you know the names of each person in the meeting since you'll need to note who is tasked with completing each agreed follow-up action item.
- During the meeting if you're not sure what is being agreed, ask for the person speaking or the entire group to clarify the agreed action.
- Ensure that with each agreed action it is clearly stated who needs to complete the task and what the deadline for completion is.
- If an action item is complicated or difficult to complete, ask the person tasked with completing it if they have any extra points that they'd like to add to the action item wording. They might need a colleague's help, or propose that they share a progress update by a certain date.
- It's common to write a meeting's follow-up actions in an email to circulate to those who attended the meeting.
- If someone missed the meeting but still had tasks allocated to them, make sure you speak with them after the meeting to walk them through what they've been asked to do.
- Don't allow yourself to take on too many of the actions, particularly if you feel someone else is better placed to complete some of those tasks.

STRETCH YOUR GOALS

If you know you can easily reach the moon, aim for Mars instead.

When creating goals and objectives for yourself and other people, do you like to be conservative and set goals you know you'll easily achieve or demand more of yourself and set stretch goals that you don't expect to fully meet? The logic of creating stretch goals is that you're setting hard or impossible-to-reach objectives in order to try to encourage yourself and your team to leave your comfort zones and to push boundaries to find out how close you can get to your challenging goals.

Research provides mixed results on the impact of stretch goals:

- Some research shows the positive impact. Dr Saeedeh Ahmadi at Rotterdam's Erasmus University studied the impact of stretch goals within a Fortune 500 tech company and found that stretch goals encourage people to be more innovative, and to brainstorm and create more ideas and possible solutions.
- On the other hand, there are studies showing that stretch goals have a negative impact. A 2017 study by Michael Shayne Gary et al., published in the journal *Organization Science*, found that people weren't committed to or motivated to try to achieve stretch goals and they performed sub-optimally and in 80 per cent of cases failed to reach them.

It's all about context. Sometimes it's sensible to set some very demanding goals, particularly if there's no other option, such as when your business's survival depends upon it; at other times it would be counterproductive and wouldn't be of any help to set goals that aren't achievable. When you're trying to increase productivity, it's up to you to make a judgement call on whether stretch or achievable goals are more likely to work best in your situation.

Set two levels of goals

Goals are simply a tool to help you maximize your performance. They are requests made by someone – by you when setting your own goals, by your boss, or maybe by your client.

All goals should be helpful for you in some way. They should give you direction, the ability to plan, and increased motivation. If a goal won't help you perform well, you'll probably ignore it. When you give team members, colleagues or suppliers goals, make sure they're motivating and clear and if they're hard to achieve, be ready to explain why you created them and how you'll help achieve them.

Consider creating two levels of goals:

- **Higher-level and longer-term goals**: these can be challenging and a stretch to achieve. They could serve to set the direction you want to aim for, and align with your vision and purpose.
- **Immediate short-term goals:** these will align with the longer-term goal but could be more achievable and something you can plan your time and resources around.

MAKE LEARNING A PRIORITY

Learn, learn more and keep on learning.

Improving your productivity is only possible through continual learning. You should always be looking to acquire new habits, ways of working, techniques, productivity hacks, processes and updates to procedures. Highly productive people typically learn in two directions – they deepen their knowledge of those areas they're already familiar with, and at the same time they broaden their knowledge of topics that are new to them.

Reading is of course a great way to achieve this, and productive people read a lot:

- The Investor Warren Buffett has been quoted as saying that he reads 500 pages a day.
- Microsoft's co-founder Bill Gates reads on average 50 books a year.
- The motivational speaker and author Tony Robbins took a speed-reading course in his youth and read 700 books in seven years.

There are many other learning tools and mediums you can use if you're not a book reader:

- speaking with mentors, coaches and colleagues
- reading magazines, newsletters and blogs
- listening to audiobooks and podcasts
- subscribing to online training resources providers such as Udemy, Coursera and LinkedIn Learning
- attending conferences, symposiums, talks and seminars
- learning on the job and through ad-hoc tasks and projects
- formal learning through colleges, institutes and professional bodies
- learning through the metaverse of virtual reality, AI and avatars.

Know your learning style

If you want to learn effectively, align your learning with how you like to learn. There's little point in buying a pile of books on a topic you want to master when you find reading so tedious and boring.

Think about your preferred learning style. Is it reading, watching videos, listening to audio files or doing an activity? To help you answer this question, you could take an assessment test. Examples of well-known online tests are the Honey and Mumford, Kolb and VAK learning styles ones. These assessments will indicate how you prefer to take in new information.

Focus on what's essential

Start by focusing your time on learning what's essential for you to succeed in your work today and over the next few years. After you've got into the flow of this type of learning, you could expand your areas of learning to cover topics, issues and subjects that really interest you but don't relate to your normal scope of work.

Experiment with learning options

Armed with the knowledge of what you want to learn and how you prefer to learn, tailor your learning strategy by trying out various learning sources (including those examples listed on the previous page) to discover which work best for you.

KEEP YOUR LAPTOP ORGANIZED

Don't live in fear of your computer crashing – use foolproof backup and filing systems.

Many of us live on our laptops and PCs, and our working days are about reading documents and emails, typing replies, creating and updating files. We've already explored how unproductive a messy and disorganized work environment can be and this also applies to what you store on your computer.

If you're well organized and efficient, you won't be wasting hours sifting through online files looking for a particular document. In a 2012 global survey by IDC of those working in the information and IT sectors (including in the UK and USA), it was discovered that on average each professional lost up to two hours per week searching for lost documents, and they had to spend an additional couple of hours each week recreating those same documents. You may not be losing as much time as these IT professionals, but how often do you struggle to find something you know is saved somewhere but just can't remember where?

Sometimes the problem might be even bigger. The file isn't just misplaced, it's lost through a hardware malfunction, losing a laptop and finding the backup files are out of date, saving a new file over an old file with the same name, a computer virus. The impact can be devastating. I know of an author who was drafting a new book on her PC, and one day she found that a virus had wiped out her entire hard drive. She had no recent backup of her data and had to start typing her manuscript again from scratch.

Chapter 73

Switch to the Cloud

The easy way to remove the fear of your laptop crashing or being stolen is simply not to store any photos, documents and important files on it – or if you do, to have backups stored online.

- Rather than using tools such as Microsoft Office that sit on your computer, use their online versions. When you do that, as soon as you start creating a Word file or Excel spreadsheet it'll be automatically saved online.
- Similarly with your photos, videos and other documents, you can automatically save them online using services such as Dropbox, Google Drive or Apple's iCloud. They're free for smaller amounts of data; you would need to pay a monthly or annual subscription fee to store larger amounts.

Pay to protect yourself

Create passwords for your apps and services that are hard to guess, and never use a single password for many of your different access logins. It's better that you forget a password and need to create a new one than a hacker guesses it.

Invest in highly rated security software to protect you against all forms of hacking and data loss including phishing and malware. Don't be fooled by free security software offerings. Subscribe to a paid service where your PC will regularly receive the latest security patches and updates.

Align when sharing

When using shared folders and directories at work, agree some shared rules, particularly on where files will be located and how they will be named. File names should follow an agreed pattern so that any of you can create and easily locate them.

ENSURE OTHERS ARE PRODUCTIVE

Share your productivity hacks with your colleagues so that when you learn, everyone gets a lift.

Productivity is a team game and sustainable high performance is a shared responsibility. Long-term success depends upon having very open and collaborative relationships with your colleagues. Share your ideas for improved performance with your peers because you'll never fully optimize your performance by being an 'island of productivity' if those around you are missing out.

Productive people appreciate that 'what goes around comes around'. You help others today and tomorrow a colleague will share their great idea with you. As well as helping other people, you'll raise your own status by being seen as innovative and generous. That can have a positive impact on your personal brand and career.

One way productive people share their experiences and ideas for improved performance is normally by being mentors, and when appropriate helping their colleagues through:

- coaching and supporting
- teaching and explaining
- on-the-job sharing and showing
- presenting in a meeting or training
- creating manuals and guides
- sharing in an email or memo
- through one-on-one catch-ups.

Mentor others

Just as you learned the benefits of having your own mentor in Chapter 57, you should consider becoming a mentor yourself so that you can pass on your own experiences to those you're working with. This will involve you:

- being a positive role model who continually sets a great example
- inviting others to watch you in action and to learn from you while you work on tasks together
- offering to share your own experiences, advice and ideas – not by lecturing and telling colleagues what to do, but by making sure that your ideas align with your colleagues' contexts and needs
- supporting them by offering to watch them in action or to review the results of their efforts
- offering to coach them if they struggle to change their working style, habits and behaviours – coaching involves inviting them to explore their issues through you asking appropriate questions, listening well and not giving them your opinions or advice
- organizing training sessions, writing 'how to' manuals or procedures, or producing a video for your colleagues to refer to.

When sharing your wisdom, always remember that just because a tool works well for you in your work it may not have the same impact when used by other people in their contexts.

AVOID EXCESSIVE SCREEN TIME

Computers, smartphones and the internet are both a blessing and a curse.

Most of us need to spend hours on our computers in order to be productive, but paradoxically spending so much time on a laptop or smartphone can be terrible for productivity:

- Too much time at a computer screen is bad for your eyes and that impacts your ability to work well. A 2020 study published in the *Indian Journal of Ophthalmology* found that those who spent more time staring at their computers and smartphones had an increased risk of eye strain, which can lead to blurred vision, headaches and an inability to concentrate.
- Internet addiction impacts both your immediate productivity as well as your mental health. Referred to as internet addiction disorder, it's a growing problem, particularly impacting those under the age of 29.
- Too much time online affects your sleep, with a 2014 study published in the *Proceedings of the National Academy of Sciences* concluding that those who read an e-book before bed took longer to fall asleep and had worse sleep than those who read printed books.
- Excessive social media use can cause depression and anxiety according to a 2018 study published in the *American Journal of Health Behavior*.

For maximum productivity, you need to be aware of these risks and try to find a balance between working online and stepping away from your PC and smartphone as often as you possibly can.

Chapter **75**

Take some precautions

Help your eyes by taking some of the following precautions:

- Follow the 20:20:20 rule – every 20 minutes, stop working and stare at something that's at least 20 feet (6 metres) away from you. Do this for at least 20 seconds. Learn more about this concept and variation of it by searching online.
- Try to minimize the glare from your computer screen by investing in the latest screen, or use a protective filter that you hang on the front of your screen.
- Make an effort to blink as often as possible to stop your eyes drying out. If they do become dry, use eye drops.
- Try wearing blue light blocking or computer glasses to help your eyes.
- Sit so that you are an arm's length (about 60cm) away from your screen.

Assess if you're addicted

Take an online assessment to help you understand the level of your internet addiction. Two of the better-known assessment tools are:

- Problematic Internet Use Questionnaire
- Compulsive Internet Use Scale.

If your addiction is hard to shake off, seek professional help from a therapist or a support group.

Control your time online

Use a work-only smartphone and computer when working, and don't install your social media on these devices. Block your access to non-work-related websites, particularly those that you know you spend time visiting.

When conducting searches online avoid spending too long aimlessly browsing through different webpages. Remain focused on what you need to find and once you've found it stop browsing.

When not working, try to rest your eyes and your brain, and limit your access to the internet (granted this is particularly hard now that we're used to watching TV via sites like Netflix and Amazon Prime).

GROUP TASKS TOGETHER

Your workload will feel more manageable if you start task-batching.

Your productivity will increase when you combine the same or similar tasks and complete them in one go rather than doing them at different times of the day. Grouping similar tasks is sometimes referred to as task- or time-batching.

Batching tasks enables you to be more efficient as they'll probably require similar ways of working, processing and thinking, which means you'll benefit from economies of scale. Examples of tasks that could be grouped are:

- making phone calls to clients
- creating client invoices or issuing payment receipts
- working on emails, including emptying your inbox
- setting up a range of meetings in your online scheduling system.

By working in this way, you'll save time from not having to open and re-open different tools and systems. This is borne out by research, with one University of Michigan study showing significant time savings when you stay with a similar range of tasks rather than switching between different pieces of work.

Grouping similar tasks also helps you to be more focused on completing those tasks in a consistent way. It should also help you clear your to-do list more quickly if, for example, you can take your 20–30 pending tasks and turn them into four or five batches. This makes your workload feel more manageable, which in turn gives you more confidence to complete everything, instead of feeling overwhelmed.

Chapter 76

Re-order your time and work

Re-design your to-do list so that tasks that can be completed one after the other are grouped together into sub-groups. As an example, you might decide that all those tasks relating to using your Customer Relationship Management (CRM) system, your SAP accounting software or making phone calls should be logically batched and completed together within the same time period.

You should also plan ahead, deciding which days of the week you will focus on recurring batched work. You might dedicate Mondays to one group of tasks, and focus on another batch on Wednesdays and Fridays.

Re-set other people's expectations

When grouping similar tasks together you may be changing your response times, with some tasks taking longer to be completed. For example, if your roles are to respond to customer complaints, issue invoices and mail out marketing materials to potential clients, before task-batching you might have responded as soon as each individual email or request was received – moving back and forth between creating invoices, dealing with complaints and mailing materials. When you start grouping tasks together, you'll need to decide the times of your day (or week) when you'll be working on different batches and, as a result, you'll need to adjust the response times in any service level agreements, while also informing your clients, colleagues and anyone else who'll be impacted by your new way of working.

HIRE AN ASSISTANT

Invest your time in activities that create most value and require your expertise and experience.

It's not the best use of your time to work on the myriad smaller tasks that need doing and that take you away from where your experience and expertise are really needed. Having someone to support you can really help boost your productivity. They can:

- hold you accountable, by reviewing with you what you're supposed to have done and what you still need to do, ensuring you never miss deadlines or key meetings
- manage your schedule for you by organizing your meetings and other activities
- block your calendar when needed to give you time on particular tasks, and stop you becoming overwhelmed
- act as a filter to manage who wants your time, scanning emails, taking phone calls and opening mail to determine what you need to personally deal with and what you can ignore
- represent you when you're unable to be in two places at the same time, and communicate on your behalf by having access to your email inbox
- act as a sounding board by being available to brainstorm and discuss issues and ideas you may have, including being able to review drafts of your presentations, proposals and replies etc.
- take on ad-hoc or bespoke tasks such as boosting your online presence and branding, managing your personal finances through to preparing financial spreadsheets and doing your travel planning.

Of course not everyone can simply get this kind of dedicated support, but it's worth having in your long-term plans. There are ideas for how you could get support on the following page.

Determine your needs

Think through the range of tasks you have to complete, noting which are a poor use of your time. It could be filing, creating invoices, booking air tickets or formatting documents. These are the types of tasks that you could consider giving to an assistant. Imagine if you could free up even just a few extra hours each week. How could you use that time to achieve more and become even more productive?

Find the right support

Today there are all kinds of available support to suit all levels of budget and needs:

- Hire someone as an employee, or contract a self-employed freelancer or company that provides secretarial and admin services.
- Start small by asking for only a few hours of help each month, and then grow to employ someone for a few days each week or even full-time.
- If you prefer a virtual online service, there are many available options, with firms offering virtual office and secretarial support services through emails and video calls.
- There might be potential to pool resources and pitch to your boss for shared support across the team. Getting a small piece of an underused assistant's time is better than nothing.
- When only needing some one-off and ad-hoc help, try using one of the marketplace websites such as www.freelancer.com, www.fiverr.com and www.upwork.com where freelancers offer all kinds of services from IT support and copywriting through to social media posting and book-keeping.

PICTURE WHAT YOU WANT

Visualize what you want – and then go and get it.

Visualization is an important tool in your productivity action list. It's powerful to visualize what you want to achieve, to create an image in your mind of your goals and objectives. As I draft this book, I have in my mind a picture of the fully completed and published book sitting on book shelves. Athletes visualize winning an upcoming event or race, engineers and entrepreneurs visualize the product or business they're designing or creating. Visualization helps you:

- gain the confidence to believe your goal is achievable
- focus your attention and energy on your objective
- create an inner motivation to work towards your desired outcome.

The science behind it claims that neurons in your brain interpret what you are visualizing as if it is real, which creates new neural pathways that help you to perform the necessary tasks.

Visualization doesn't have to just be for the ultimate goal, you can also visualize what you need to do to achieve the outcomes – picturing the steps you need to follow. Research suggests that this might be more effective than goal visualization itself, with a well-cited 1999 study published in the journal *Personality and Social Psychology Bulletin* being one of the first to arrive at this conclusion. A well-known example of a person doing this is the climber Alex Honnold who successfully climbed Yosemite National Park's El Capitan without ropes in 2018. Before doing so he spent many weeks visualizing his route up the 1,000-metre vertical rock face, going as far as picturing in his mind each of his planned hand and foot holds.

Create a picture

As you work on tasks, take the time to ask yourself what the ideal finished outcomes will look and feel like. Make this a daily or weekly habit which you do no matter what you want to achieve. Visualize your goal either by:

- closing your eyes and imagining in your mind what success looks and feels like, or
- creating a vision board where you draw a picture of what success looks like, or you collect pictures (from the web or magazines) and items which symbolize your desired goal.

Visualize the steps you need to take

Emulate the free solo climber Alex Honnold by planning how you'll go about completing a task or fulfilling your goal. Picture yourself actually completing the different steps. For example, this might include you visualizing yourself:

- making a successful series of phone calls to new clients that you wish to contract with
- studying well for your professional exams as part of you becoming qualified.

The ideal is to visualize both your end goal and each of the steps required to achieve it. Making this a habit won't guarantee success, but it'll be an important contributor.

FIND YOUR MOTIVATION

Follow your purpose and your passion.

Even highly productive people can only sustain their performance when they're motivated by what they are doing. This won't come as a surprise. You'll have noticed how hard work seems when motivation levels drop.

Motivation is a critical concept, but at the same time it's hard to define and measure. At its simplest, it's the extent to which you want to do, to be or to have something. Psychologists have discovered that our motivations are either intrinsic or extrinsic:

- Intrinsic motivation means you want to do something because it's inherently enjoyable or interesting. For example, you're hopefully reading this book because it interests you.
- Extrinsic motivation means you want to do something because of external rewards which are distinct from the actual activity. For example, you probably work overtime at weekends because your boss will recognize your efforts and you earn extra money.

People at the high end of the productivity spectrum typically have a clear understanding of what motivates them. They will always try to ensure that their time is spent on tasks that both intrinsically and extrinsically motivate them, doing work they enjoy and is also rewarding in terms of recognition and remuneration.

Motivation also links to ensuring that your work aligns with your passions and strengths – topics we explored in Chapter 12 and Chapter 23 respectively.

Know what drives you

Think about *why* you're doing what you're doing. Make a list of your most important responsibilities and the tasks you need to spend time on in order to be successful in your work. For each item answer the following questions:

- To what extent does this task motivate me (give it a rating out of 10)?
- What are the intrinsic and/or extrinsic motivators that are driving me to complete this task?
- How can I sustain and/or grow these existing motivators?
- In what other ways can I make this task more motivating for me?

By regularly asking yourself these questions, you'll gain an honest understanding about what is driving you. This will help you know which tasks you want to focus on and which you may no longer want to work on.

Do it anyway

If you have an important piece of work to complete but it doesn't motivate you, do it anyway. If you need to kick start your motivation try the five-second countdown attributed to US-based motivational speaker Mel Robbins. It's simple but does work. Just count down in your head from five to zero and then begin working on the task. It's like taking that first plunge into a cold swimming pool – once you're in, it's fine.

You could build on the visualization advice from the previous chapter, picturing in your mind how pleased and relieved you'll be once you've finished a dull or monotonous task. Hopefully the mental image will help motivate you to complete the task as soon as possible.

TRACK YOUR PROGRESS

If you don't track your progress, how do you know when you've succeeded?

It's not enough to set a goal and work towards it, you have to monitor your progress in order to maximize your likelihood of succeeding. This was confirmed in a 2016 University of Sheffield study reported in the journal *Psychological Bulletin*, in which researchers assessed the impact of monitoring your progress towards achieving health-related goals. They concluded that:

- the more frequently you monitor your progress, the higher the probability that you will reach your goal
- you're even more likely to succeed if you share details of your progress with other people, such as your colleagues (learn more about this in Chapter 97).

In addition to keeping you focused on your goals, reviewing your progress:

- provides a sense of achievement and an opportunity to celebrate small wins on the way to attaining your main goals
- ensures you don't lose your way and waste precious time and energy on the wrong activities.

Depending on the type of goal, productive people will use a variety of monitoring tools – either utilizing those supplied and supported by their organization or creating their own.

Chapter 80

Use tracking processes

When working within any organization, it's likely that you'll be using company-wide systems which have monitoring, check-in and reviewing processes built in, such as:

- detailed budgets, forecasts and action plans to compare your actual performance on either a daily, weekly, monthly and/or quarterly basis
- SAP, Oracle Enterprise planning and business software processes, which typically come with real-time data monitoring, progress reporting and exception reporting functionalities
- project management processes for reviewing progress, such as Gantt charts
- agile ways of working, which include daily scrum meetings with your team, where you assess issues and progress real-time.

You'll need to ensure that the required methods for tracking progress are being optimally adhered to.

Create your own monitoring processes

If no ideal monitoring process is prescribed or available for you and your team, design your own. It can be as simple as having regular team meetings, observing your own performance, creating and using checklists, forecasts, project plans or activity logs.

Depending on your types of goals and related tasks you could also try out a monitoring website such as: www.rescuetime.com, www.toggl.com and www.nTask.com.

MAINTAIN A 'NOT TO-DO' LIST

A 'not to-do' list will help you avoid filling your time with unproductive activities.

By being 100 per cent clear on what you're not going to do, you'll be better able to focus your time and energy on the important things. Whereas a traditional 'to-do' list comprises tasks with specific deadlines attached to each, your 'not to-do list' is typically made up of a mix of recurring habits, behaviours and tasks you want to avoid such as:

• distractions that stop you being productive
• things that you hate doing
• tasks that create no value
• stuff that stresses you out
• tasks that drain you
• things that are beyond your control
• actions that aren't important for you to do
• things you should always say 'no' to doing
• your unproductive habits and addictions.

There aren't any deadlines here because *none* of this is getting done any time soon. This is your daily reminder of what you need to avoid to protect your productivity. Examples of actual items on a 'not to-do' list might include:

• not checking emails every few minutes
• not always saying 'yes' to your boss's requests
• not working on reports that are your colleague's sole responsibility
• not spending time constantly multi-tasking.

Chapter 81

Create your 'not to-do' list

Work through the categories listed on the previous page by asking yourself:

- What unproductive distractions do I need to stop doing?
- What things do I hate doing?
- Which tasks create no value?
- What things stress me out?
- Which tasks drain me?
- What things are beyond my control?
- What actions aren't important to do?
- Which things should I always say 'no' to doing?
- What are my unproductive habits and addictions?

List your answers on your draft 'not to-do' list and include anything that:

- doesn't help you achieve your goals, vision or any positive value
- has been on your to-do list a long time, is still unfinished and no one seems to care or notice.

Before treating your list as final, go through each item to double check if it'll be ok for you not to do it. Ask yourself what the consequences of not completing each task are. Who would be upset or angry with you if you failed to complete them? It's ok to remove items from your 'not to-do' list to keep the peace!

Stick to it

Once you've finalized your list, stick to it by:

- printing it out and placing it in a visible location to remind you of what you're no longer prepared to spend time on
- sharing it with colleagues and asking them to keep you on track and to hold you accountable
- stopping what you're doing as soon as you find yourself doing anything that's on the list.

AVOID WORKAHOLISM

Too much of anything can be bad for you.

Being hard-working is viewed positively in society and it's a badge of honour to say that you're really busy. Having a strong work ethic is good, but do be aware of the downsides. It's easy to become so focused on your work that you slip into an unhealthy pattern, becoming addicted to producing more and more. The dangers of workaholism are real. This compulsive need to work is more than simply putting in long hours. The signs of it include:

- feeling guilty when not working on anything
- rushing through family dinners in order to get back to your work
- always putting yourself under self-imposed deadlines when you're working
- mistaking quantity for quality, and thinking that the more emails you answer or meetings you attend, the better your performance
- becoming obsessed with your own performance and productivity, and never having time to support other people
- being proud of how busy you are, for example proudly sharing how much you travel with work and telling people how many air miles you've acquired.

We all have moments of becoming consumed by our work, it's when that becomes the norm that it becomes unhealthy. If you tend towards work addiction, you're not alone. A 2014 Norwegian study found that one in twelve people fall into the category of being workaholics, while a 2019 survey in the USA, summarized in the *New York Post*, found that 48 per cent of those surveyed claimed to be workaholics.

With any addiction, the problem is that over time you need more and more to be satisfied. This means that if you don't stop yourself, your workaholic tendencies will increasingly consume you and your life, leading to broken relationships, health issues and a decline in your work performance.

Chapter 82

Are you addicted?

Try taking a test to find out how addicted you are to work. Two examples of the better-known tests are:

- the Bergen Work Addiction Scale which is based on 2014 research, published in the *Scandinavian Journal of Psychology*, and involves answering seven questions about your work habits and approach to work
- the Work Addiction Risk Test which was created in the USA in 1999 and involves answering 25 questions about your working style and habits.

You can easily search online to find free or low-cost versions of either test (or similar ones) that you could take.

Deal with workaholic tendencies

If you are working obsessively, your behaviours might simply need toning down and reducing in frequency. If you find or know your issue won't be so easily solved, then it's likely that you're dealing with a genuine addiction.

Extreme or addictive workaholism tends to have a psychological cause, such as a childhood desire to please your parents by always working hard and being the perfect student. As with other addictions, you may need the help of a therapist specializing in a process called cognitive behavioural therapy who could help you unlock the reasons and overcome the problem.

KNOW YOUR OWN CAPACITY

Your plate can only hold so much – if you keep heaping food on,
some of it will fall off.

These days we're very good at calculating a business's capacity to produce products or services. Thanks to technology, you can easily assess your department or function's processes and systems to understand their optimal capacity based on criteria such as:

• how many units of production can be manufactured each day
• how much product a warehouse can process per hour
• the quantity of reports that can be produced each week
• the length of time needed to conduct a specific audit or test.

It's natural for productive people to want to apply this same capacity for measuring and monitoring to themselves. You want to understand how much you're capable of producing, so that you can plan and set yourself realistic targets. This isn't easy to calculate since people aren't like machines whose potential output is easy to calculate. We don't work at uniform rates like a product assembly line or computer process. It's especially hard to calculate when work includes activities such as reflecting, thinking, analysing, brainstorming and decision-making.

A further complication is that we're unique and we cannot simply estimate our capacity by comparing it with others. Our different levels of natural ability, experience and skills means the same task might take each of us different amounts of time and energy to complete.

In addition to understanding their own capacity levels, productive people continually work to expand their capacity. This is like the process you follow at the gym, where each week you might push yourself to lift more weights or complete more reps.

Chapter 83

Know the real size of your plate

The following steps will help you calculate your optimal work capacity:

1 Calculate your time capacity by asking yourself how much time you are willing to spend working in a day, week or month. This might be as simple as saying you'll work for nine hours a day for five days a week.
2 Estimate how much output you can achieve within the time you'll spend working. This is harder to calculate and depends on the type of tasks you need to complete. Start by observing what you produce over a number of days or weeks, and ask yourself, were you very busy or was your team being underutilized?
3 Decide if your current level of performance can be repeated on a sustainable basis. There's little point in working for over 15 hours a day over an entire week (on an urgent project) and then committing with your boss that you will sustain this level of performance moving forward.

You may struggle to arrive at a precise calculation of your optimal work capacity, but try to get enough of a sense so that you can always know when:

• you have spare capacity to accept extra tasks
• you're reaching the limits of your capacity and need to slow down, push back and negotiate timeframes.

By regularly observing and reviewing yourself you'll become more proficient at knowing the limits of what you can optimally handle.

Make your plate larger

When trying to expand your capacity, do so in effective and sustainable ways through a combination of:

• building up your knowledge and skills level
• taking on new tasks
• doing things in new and smarter ways
• optimizing your health, sleep and work environment
• eliminating unnecessary tasks, wasted and down time.

ALWAYS DO THE RIGHT THINGS RIGHT

It's not enough just to do the right tasks, you must do them in the right way.

Excellence is all about continually achieving two connected things: ensuring that you're focusing on achieving the right goals and outcomes, while also making sure that you are working towards them in the right way. To use a travel analogy:

- There's little point in travelling very efficiently, cost-effectively and quickly if you're heading in the wrong direction.
- Similarly, when you're heading in the right direction, you'd be wasting your time if you chose to drive in a poorly maintained car that broke down along the way.

Too many people choose the ideal tools and tasks but then fail to follow through effectively by using the tools badly and not completing the tasks well. This could be laziness, forgetfulness, lack of focus or just busyness. As an example, it's not enough to:

- use a well-designed to-do list when you don't keep it updated or refer to it on a regular basis
- delegate work to the right colleagues but then give them incomplete guidance on what to do or forget to follow up with them
- separate important incoming emails into useful sub-folders and then forget to read and answer all of them
- hold effective meetings but forget to circulate meeting minutes with agreed actions.

Being productive is about doing the right things well all the time. Simply knowing what to do is only half the battle. To be productive you need to match knowledge with execution.

Use a structured approach

To be sure of completing any task as perfectly as possible, work through the following six pieces of interconnected advice. This list is collectively known as Gilbert's Six Boxes and it's a tool often used in the human resources field, based on the 1970s' work of the US academic Thomas Gilbert. When you optimally work through all six areas, you can be assured of being able to complete any task well:

1 Obtain the right information and feedback to help you know what to do. This might involve having a written job role or guidelines explaining what needs to be done and why. Ask yourself if you also need more informal or formal feedback to help you.

2 Have the ideal tools, processes and resources to optimally complete the task. Sometimes it's as simple as exchanging your old PC for a newer and faster one.

3 Explore if you have the ideal incentives to motivate and push you to achieve more and to exceed expectations. Perhaps you need to request a bigger incentive.

4 Ensure you have the ideal skills and knowledge to enable you to excel. It may not be enough to simply attend a relevant training course or to obtain appropriate work experience – you also need to know how to use what you've learned.

5 Ask if you have the ability, time and overall capacity to do what is asked of you. Seek help if a task leaves you struggling and out of your depth.

6 Work to build up and create the ideal levels of motivation and commitment to be able to complete the task well.

As well as using this six-part framework with your own task completion, it can be used with any team you lead.

MAKE FRIENDS WITH AI

Embrace the potential of AI technology to re-design your work.

Artificial intelligence (AI) is coming and we're all going to feel the impact. It's not necessarily something to fear. One of the over-riding benefits will be to make us more productive through having our jobs re-designed and re-defined. We'll be free to focus on where we bring most value and tasks that require our skills and experience.

In research reported in the May 2018 papers and proceedings of the American Economic Association, researchers from MIT concluded that AI will lead to the re-design of jobs and reengineering of business practices, rather than purely eliminating jobs.

Research and surveys all point to a future where AI will impact all aspects of our work and non-work lives, with a 2021 PwC survey finding that 86 per cent of organizations report that AI is already a key or mainstream technology across their business. It's helping us to work more productively in many ways, including:

- crunching data and finding patterns and trends which we otherwise might miss
- making better decisions through bringing data together more effectively
- forecasting numbers and trends more accurately than we could alone
- scanning files and documents to help us find relevant information and patterns.

The secret to success is to accept and embrace the relentless growth of AI in our workplaces and our lives, and to use it to help maximize performance and productivity.

Have an open mind

No job description remains unchanged for long. There is a possibility that developments in AI might make some parts of your job redundant but rather than fearing the worst, embrace the potential of technology to re-design your work.

Building on what we covered in Chapter 11, become a super-user, keen to try out new intelligent technologies as they become available in your workplace to explore how they can make you more productive. Some may help you work faster, others will dispense with your tedious and repetitive tasks or help you to complete tasks which would otherwise be impossible to do.

Explore how AI can help you today

The quickest and easiest place to start is on your laptop. Think through what you need to do on your computer, asking yourself which pieces of recurring work are the most time consuming and/or most difficult and complicated. Then do an online search to find which AI-based solutions might be the perfect productivity hacks for you to try.

- Perhaps you struggle with written communication, so find an online automatic English editing tool, to help you produce high-quality written emails and reports.
- If you're slow at typing, try a solution that turns your voice recordings into written text.
- If you want to know which colleagues or clients you connect with most often, find an online tool to monitor your main contacts, based on how often you email and message each of them.

MAKE WORK FUN AND ENJOYABLE

If you enjoy your job, you'll never have to work another day in your life.

Having fun at work is proven to be good for your work performance:

- In a 2020 study published in the *Journal of Vocational Behavior*, researchers in Norway found that when employees create conditions that foster joy, their job performance improves.
- A 2017 study, published in the *Journal of Management*, reviewed available research and found that fun and play at work are linked with reduced tiredness, stress and burnout, and with increased levels of creativity, engagement, trust and job satisfaction.
- Fun and play are linked to happiness, and a 2015 study from the University of Warwick concluded that happier employees are more productive by between 12 and 20 per cent.

We're all unique and some high performers might feel distracted by a work environment filled with moments of fun, laughter and play. You might know the kind of colleague I'm referring to – never stopping to chat or to take part in social events. They may be performing well, but they could do even better if they let themselves have some fun.

Thankfully most people prefer and perform better when there are some light-hearted moments. It's contagious too – even the grumpiest colleague finds it hard not to smile and giggle when colleagues around them start laughing. It's easy and free to create fun moments. It could be as simple as having a radio playing in your office, or sharing some funny stories over a coffee break or at the start of a team meeting.

Chapter 86

Stop being so serious

If you're the type of person who never wants to mix work with play, then it's time you changed and loosened up – for the sake of your productivity!

• Smile and laugh during the working day.
• Wear work clothes that you enjoy and make you feel good.
• Join colleagues for lunch or after-work drinks.
• Celebrate colleagues' birthdays and other special moments.
• Take time to share fun stories and jokes.
• Organize team-building events.

Be inclusive

Fun and enjoyment at work can take many forms and one person's idea of a fun time may not be another's. It's important that you try to create activities that everyone in your office will find positive. Compromise is the key.

Bring fun to every meeting

Meetings don't have to be exempt. We spend so much of our time in them and they're often serious and tense. To offset this, why not start every meeting with an ice-breaker activity. Ask everyone to answer a question such as:

• If you could visit any country in the world, where would you go?
• If your life was made into a Hollywood blockbuster movie, what would its title be?
• What is the one thing you're most proud of achieving in the last year (or in your life)?

USE ONLINE TOOLS AND APPS

There are online solutions for every conceivable productivity challenge.

Online tools can make all the difference to your productivity. High performers know this, and most, if not all, are becoming tech savvy and comfortable using the growing range of online tools and apps on their laptops and smartphones. They're constantly searching out different online tools to find an edge in managing their working and personal lives.

Do you need to do any of these?

- write and store notes and ideas
- prioritize tasks during the working day
- show how long you've been working on different tasks
- interact in real-time on shared documents with colleagues
- deal with a long and ever-changing to-do list
- share information and files with others
- communicate more effectively with colleagues
- schedule meetings and events.

The secret is to explore and experiment with apps and tools on your laptop and smartphone, while also working optimally with your organization's shared online systems and tools.

Chapter 87

Find what works for you

Explore the extensive and growing selection of online apps and web-based tools to find out which will help boost your productivity and work performance. Below I've listed a selection of some highly rated ones below to get you started. I've grouped them according to the primary way they've been designed to help you become more productive, but many of them can Below I've listed help you in more ways than one. Take the time to learn about some of them and try them out.

To help create and manage to-do lists:

- Airtable
- Look Habit Tracker
- Monday
- Process.st
- Serene
- Taskade
- Todoist
- Trello
- WeDo
- Wunderlist

To help manage your time:

- Be Focused
- Due
- Engross
- Forest
- Habitica
- Things 3
- Toggl

To help you schedule your work and tasks:

- Any.do
- Doodle
- Calendar
- Calendly

To help you share and collaborate:

- Google Docs
- Hive
- Loom
- Mural
- Notion
- Pocket
- Slack
- Teams
- Trello
- Zoom

For messaging with colleagues:

- Line
- Viber
- Wechat
- WhatsApp

MAKE TIME

Don't focus on certain tasks at the expense of others.

When you take a closer look into people's habits and behaviours, you'll find that many perform well in one part of their work and lives but neglect other areas. You might know of people who:

- work on one project for hours to the detriment of their other priorities
- spend hours in meetings and never answer their phone or emails
- focus on new assignments and never make time to finish existing tasks
- are in the office for ten hours a day and neglect their family's evening commitments
- become engrossed in tasks and rarely stop for lunch or to exercise.

As we saw in Chapter 6, it's fine to neglect activities that are low in importance, but something's wrong if a single-minded focus on a single priority leads to neglect of other important tasks. Making time for all of your important work and non-work commitments is critical. You should make a single to-do list for all of your work and non-work activities, creating groups or buckets of tasks such as:

Work-related groups of tasks – covering:	Non-work-related groups of tasks – covering:
Current/daily work	Exercise
Project X	Housework
Project Y	Family time
Strategy review	Volunteering
Hiring new staff	Health

You can then allocate a percentage of your upcoming week to each group of tasks. Dividing up your week (or even month) in this way compels you to balance out how you focus your time and energy, and ensures that nothing gets forgotten because you never allocated any time to it.

Allocate time to each bucket

Create your own to-do list containing all your work and non-work-related tasks. Place each task into a range of appropriate sub-groupings or buckets as in the example on the previous page.

Focus first on the work-related buckets. Decide what percentage of your working week you need to spend on each and then block time in your calendar in line with the percentages. Based on the example from the previous page this breakdown of your week might look like this:

Buckets of tasks	% of time (during week)	When is calendar blocked?
Tasks related to current work	50%	Monday, Wednesday afternoon, Thursday and Friday morning
Project X	20%	All of Tuesday
Project Y	10%	Wednesday morning
Strategy review	10%	Friday afternoon
Hiring new staff	10%	2–4 interviews spread over week
Total	100%	

You can create a similar breakdown of how you want to use your free time so that you can complete all of your non-work-related buckets, ensuring none is forgotten about.

You'll need to have the self-control to ensure that:

• you don't over-work on one group of tasks, forgetting to switch to another in line with your planned schedule
• your work-related tasks don't overflow or impinge on the time you've set aside for non-work-related tasks.

DON'T LET OTHERS STEAL YOUR TIME

After your health, your time is your most valuable asset.

Earlier chapters have covered ideas and tools for optimally managing the 24 hours in your day – from getting enough sleep, to having effective meetings through to not working on trivial activities. But you also need to stop other people stealing your time. This can happen when your colleagues:

- continually interrupt you with trivial questions and requests
- don't read your emails or listen in meetings, meaning you have to repeat your instructions or requests
- cc you in emails which you then need to skim read only to realize that they're of no relevance to you at all
- invite you to meetings without telling you why or sharing an agenda with you
- create unnecessary tensions, conflicts and misunderstandings which waste your time and energy
- don't plan their work well, forcing you to step in and work overtime to ensure deadlines are met.

To be as productive as you want to be, you should never allow people to waste your time. 'Once bitten, twice shy' is a good proverb. You may be dragged into a long and useless meeting once, or over-rely on a colleague who doesn't do what they promised, but don't let it become a repeat occurrence.

Chapter 89

Don't be fooled twice

Don't allow colleagues to repeat time-stealing behaviours with you:

• When you attend a meeting which turns out to have been a waste of your time, be very careful about accepting future meeting invitations from the same person and consider asking them why they're inviting you.

• When someone agrees to do something for you but does it badly or not at all, be wary of relying on them again.

Sometimes people don't realize that they're wasting your time, perhaps because no one has ever given them this feedback. By sharing your frustrations and disappointments with them, they'll hopefully get the message.

Protect your diary

If you work in an organization where you're able to see each other's online calendars and schedules, you might block chunks of your own calendar up to a couple of weeks in advance. These would be periods of your working week that are protected.

Similarly, when colleagues randomly interrupt you with a question, don't allow yourself to be side-tracked in that moment (unless of course it's an emergency situation). Check what they want to talk about and politely but firmly say you're currently busy and suggest speaking later.

WORK ON YOUR OWN SOMETIMES

If you're in a hurry to get things done, work on your own.

Most people find they're more productive working on their own. According to 2008 research from the University of Calgary, we complete our work faster in isolation compared to working with colleagues around. Researchers found that witnessing people or being aware of people around you performing different tasks is distracting and slows you down. Research in 2020, summarized in the *Harvard Business Review*, found that knowledge workers were more productive working alone from home compared to working in their offices. They spent 12 per cent less time being drawn into unproductive meetings and were able to spend 9 per cent more time connecting with their customers and other important external stakeholders.

Working alone means you can work in silence, which brings its own proven productivity benefits:

- A 2013 study, published in the journal *Brain Structure and Function*, found that periods spent in silence promote the cell development in the part of our brain, the hippocampus, related to memory.
- In 2021 research published in the journal *Indoor Air* concluded that those who work in silence experience less stress and cognitive overload.

Hiding away and working alone can bring enormous productivity benefits so always try to build in time away from other people. Just don't get isolated. There are many times when you need to physically interact with other people on tasks that require collaborative sharing and discussion.

Chapter 90

Become comfortable working in isolation

If you're an introvert you might already be maximizing the time you get to work by yourself, using empty meeting rooms or working from home where possible. If you're an extrovert though, this might be more of a struggle. Extroverts get their energy from interacting with other people so can find it hard to work alone for extended periods. Fortunately, using alone time to increase productivity isn't about being a hermit. Just be prepared, as a minimum, to work alone when completing tasks that:

- require intense focus and concentration
- involve reading and reflecting on a lot of written material
- are complicated and detailed, where any distractions would be disruptive to your workflow.

Create an isolated work area

Try the following tips to create space where you can work alone:

- If you have your own office, shut the door.
- If you work in a noisy and open plan work area, find an empty room or if that's not possible, simply the quietest space you can.
- If you can't get away from your work station, just let your colleagues know that you need to concentrate and how long you expect to need. Try wearing some headphones without any sound on – or even noise cancelling – to create the impression that you cannot be interrupted.

DON'T CHEAT

Cutting corners is no way to win a race.

There's a right way and a wrong way to achieve your goals. You might have experienced colleagues who:

- pretend they've completed a task when they haven't even started it yet
- take credit for other people's work and ideas
- fail to follow processes and systems, leading to quality, safety or governance issues
- cover up mistakes they've made which can later cause all kinds of issues for other people who rely upon their outputs to complete their own work
- make fictitious excuses and blame other people for their own mistakes and errors of judgement
- give or receive bribes from suppliers or clients
- share and spread lies about other people's behaviours, actions or performance
- cheat and lie in all kinds of documentation – from their expense claim forms through to their daily timesheets.

A genuinely successful high performer will never stoop to such behaviour. They'll always try to perform to the highest standards. They'll openly apologize when they make mistakes. They'll hold themselves and their organization up to the highest ethical standards. People can get away with things in the short term but they'll always be found out eventually. So stay on the right path. Keep your integrity. Be productive, don't just seem to be productive.

Reflect on your values and standards

When under pressure to achieve your goals, it can be tempting to cut a few corners. Could you see yourself doing this? You can review your ethical stance by taking an online assessment test and comparing your answers to the range of responses. Some free online ethics-focused assessments include:

- Moment of Truth: Ethics Assessment (https://quiz.tryinteract.com/#/5ba94 b62d60509001343dd10)
- PMI Ethics Self-Assessment (https://www.pmi.org/-/media/pmi/documents/ public/pdf/ethics/ethics-self-assessment.pdf?v=b8c50e98-936f-4b14-9f53-ae1d50fe4afc)
- Psychology Today Integrity and Work Ethics Test (https://www.psychology-today.com/gb/tests/career/integrity-and-work-ethics-test).

After completing a test, reflect on your results to make sure your ethical standards are where you'd expect or hope them to be.

Always follow the rules

There are written and unwritten integrity and ethics-related rules you should be abiding by including:

- applicable legislation existing in your country such as the US's Foreign Corrupt Practices Act or the UK's Bribery Act (2010)
- a formal employee handbook, code of ethics or code of conduct that exists within your organization, profession and/or industry sector
- accepted ways of working in your organization such as if you make a mistake, you always come clean and immediately tell your line manager.

The bottom line is, if you want to be a highly productive and successful person, do it in the right way. And don't be a dick.

RECORD UNEXPECTED IDEAS

Capture your lightbulb moments – they can supercharge your performance.

Being productive involves continually thinking through all kinds of questions, issues, scenarios and problems, and then coming up with answers and solutions. These answers might come to you quickly – in a team meeting where the problem is actually being discussed or while reading an email describing the challenge that needs solving – but that's not always the case. Sometimes the best ideas only come to you later and often at the most inopportune moments – when you're out walking the dog, in the shower, or when you sit bolt upright at 3am with a fully-formed answer. According to the UK's Barclays Bank, the most common time for a small business owner to come up with a new business idea is 2:33am, with over half (57 per cent) of the respondents to their survey admitting to having woken up in the middle of the night with ideas on their mind.

Lightbulb moments come at random times – most often when you've moved on from the question you're trying to resolve and your brain continues quietly working on it in the background. This isn't always convenient but let's just take a moment to marvel at how great our brains are.

A good productivity technique is to know that these flashes of inspiration will come and to prepare for them by finding ways of recording them so that when you're back in work mode you can easily access them again.

Develop a way of easily recording ideas

There are many ways to record your lightbulb moments. You can be traditional and write down or draw your ideas:

- Keep a notepad and pen by your bed or in your bathroom.
- Have a small whiteboard or blackboard in your kitchen or study.
- Carry a journal and pen with you when travelling.

Alternatively, embrace technology and use your smartphone or tablet to capture your insights:

- SMS or email to write a message to yourself
- a voice memo app to verbally record your insight
- typing in a note-taking app such as Note2Self, Deepstash or Google Keep, or
- using a search engine to look for an image or webpage that'll help you recall the idea (which you can take a screenshot of to be able to refer to later).

Empty your mind to make space

Even more important than recording your lightbulb moments though is to encourage more moments of unexpected insight to come to you. To do this, learn to calm and empty your mind. The easiest way to achieve this is by regularly doing one or more of the following practices:

- yoga and breathing exercises
- meditating or praying
- avoiding watching TV or using your phone before bed
- reading relaxing and inspiring books or articles
- listening to calming and relaxing music
- getting a good night's sleep
- avoiding alcohol or other drugs
- walking in nature.

CHOOSE FRIENDS WISELY

Productive people gravitate towards individuals with qualities they
want to emulate.

There's an idea that we are the sum of our five closest friends. This makes
sense. You're strongly influenced by the people you spend most time with and
their behaviours and mindsets rub off on you. So, if you want to become more
productive you should associate with productive people and successful role
models. Research confirms this:

- The late Harvard psychologist Dr David McClelland is widely cited as concluding that those we spend most time with determine up to 95 per cent of
  the successes and failures in our lives.
- In a study published in the journal *Psychological Science* in 2013, researchers found that spending time with strong-willed people boosts our own
  willpower and self-control.

Be selective about who you include in your inner circle, who you seek as mentors and who you spend most of your time with at work and in your social
life. Productive people are drawn to individuals with qualities they want to
emulate such as:

- persistence
- determination
- focus
- ambition
- structure
- empathy
- ethical views
- honesty.

Try to avoid spending time with anyone who drains you or has a negative
influence on you.

Chapter 93

Spend time with highly productive people

Spend more time with people who support you and believe in your desire to become more successful in your work and career.

Avoid toxic colleagues, family and friends

Stop spending time with people who bring you down and make it harder for you to grow and improve. It's difficult enough to succeed in life, but it's made so much harder when you're in the company of destructive people who:

• drain your energy
• demotivate you
• ridicule and criticize your goals and ideas
• are lazy and disorganized
• belittle and put you down
• are jealous of you
• don't have your interests at heart
• actively undermine you
• blame and criticize you behind your back
• withhold help and support.

There is no need to upset them by having some big break-up. Just spend less time with them. Find excuses to be occupied when they invite you out and avoid having long conversations with them in your office.

TAKE CARE WORKING IN GROUPS

Don't just blindly follow the crowd – they might be heading in the wrong direction.

As we've seen, being productive is more than a solo pursuit. Your performance depends on working optimally within teams. When you do this well the results can be amazing. You're more productive, motivated, creative, harder working and engaged as a result of team members collaborating, sharing, supporting, helping each other.

The benefits of working in teams have been well researched. A well-known 2014 Stanford study, published in the *Journal of Experimental Social Psychology*, found that compared to those who worked alone, the study's participants who worked on tasks in teams:

- continued with their tasks longer and achieved better results
- reported being less tired and more engaged
- were more motivated to take on challenges due to the mere feeling or perception of being in a team.

When working within a team, try to sustain these positive benefits while minimizing any potential downsides which include:

- falling into the trap of groupthink – flowing with a group decision or consensus even if some of the team know it is incorrect
- some people do work better alone, and struggle to align and interact when working with others
- energy and time wasted on team dynamics issues such as personality clashes, blame games and poor communication
- unbalanced workloads – some team members free-riding and being lazy while others have too much to do and are forced to over-work.

Chapter 94

Follow the rules

Follow these essential teamworking rules to ensure that whenever you're working in a team, the teamworking and team environment boost your productivity:

- Strengthen relationships and trust – to reach your full collective potential, you and your colleagues need to know each other really well and build up high levels of trust.
- Align on purpose and values – it's important to agree on where you're all heading as a team and how you'll work together, in terms of your common team values.
- Understand each other's roles, goals and strengths – it's far easier to work productively when you appreciate one another's job responsibilities, key performance indicators as well as each other's strengths and weaknesses.
- Create a collaborative sharing culture – continually help and support each another in order to capitalize on team synergies.
- Make excellent collective decisions – it's important that all voices and opinions are always heard and shared, with team members being comfortable challenging and criticizing one another.
- Avoid games and time-wasting – never waste your valuable time being pulled into gossip sessions, playing office politics or in useless team meetings.
- Regularly review how you're working together as a team – collect feedback and agree to implement any helpful suggestions about how you can all operate more successfully as a team.

TALK MORE FACE TO FACE

Verbal, face-to-face communication is vital for enhancing productivity.

There's a widespread belief that putting a message in writing is quicker, more efficient and less awkward than picking up the phone. That's why we all tend to over-rely on sending emails rather than communicating verbally. This is wrong. Research shows that relying on emails, memos and messenger apps damages your personal standing, relationships and productivity.

- You are more easily misunderstood when communicating in writing. A 2021 survey commissioned by the UK company Hidden Hearing found that we often waste time struggling to decipher text messages. In the survey, one third of the respondents said that they had fallen out with someone simply because they had misread a text message.
- Speaking may be more effective than writing for persuasion. In a 2017 study, published in the *Journal of Experimental Social Psychology*, researchers concluded that we overestimate our ability to convince and explain when communicating via writing, while underestimating how persuasive we are when talking. One of the reasons given was a lack of personal connection and empathy felt by others when relying on written messages.
- Speaking rather than sending written messages creates a stronger relationship between people. In 2020 research from the *University of Texas at Austin*, researchers concluded that speaking with people creates stronger bonds and connections than relying on written messages. The same study found that people preferred sending texts or emails because they felt it was less awkward than speaking.
- When you want someone to like you and accept your ideas and opinions, you can easily fail when communicating in writing, since according to Professor Albert Mehrabian at UCLA we tend to like people more by how they look and sound rather than based on their choice of words.

Face-to-face communication is hugely important for enhancing productivity. Always try to talk in person (or online or over the phone) rather than relying upon an email or WhatsApp discussion.

Chapter 95

Talk in person

When you have a short message or a few words to share with a colleague or business partner, give them a call. It'll give your message a human touch and it's an opportunity to briefly connect. You can always follow up with a short email to confirm what you discussed.

The following are more situations where communicating in person rather than through a written medium will be more effective:

- **Sharing difficult news:** when you need to give a colleague or team member some critical feedback it's better to share it verbally rather than in writing. Written feedback can appear cold and can easily be misunderstood. By sharing in person you're able to see and feel the person's reactions and respond accordingly.
- **Following up on written requests:** when emailing instructions, a plan of action or any kind of complicated request, follow up your message with a spoken conversation. Talking together, even on the phone, enables you to check you've been understood and allows the other party to ask questions, share their concerns, and if necessary, push back and negotiate with you. This sort of conversation would take so much longer by email.
- **Making time for regular catch-ups:** meeting together enables you to discuss issues and topics in a faster and more efficient way than in long email chains. Keep team gatherings short, and follow the effective meeting best practices from Chapter 22 and Chapter 70.

INVEST IN YOU

You won't achieve your full potential if you don't invest in yourself.

Productive people know that their future success depends on their investment in productivity-enhancing tools and solutions. These will normally fall into the following categories:

- **Health**: see Chapter 4 for the importance of keeping fit and healthy to become highly productive.
- **Work environment**: see Chapter 30 for the importance of having an ergonomic work station, and Chapter 54 for the benefits of creating an optimal work area.
- **Support network**: as we explored in Chapter 10, you may need other people to help you by taking some of your workload off your shoulders.
- **Tools**: there may be hardware, software and online solutions that you need to boost your productivity.
- **Processes and systems**: investment may be required to automate manual processes or to take advantage of AI solutions (a topic we explored in Chapter 85).
- **Learning**: see Chapter 72 for how acquiring new skills and knowledge is key to performing well and to remaining productive.

Chapter **96**

Invest in all needed areas

Work through this table to give you some ideas of where you may need to invest in yourself to help boost your performance and productivity:

Area of focus	Examples of productivity-enhancing purchases
Your health	Consume food and drink which helps your energy levels and brain functioning Have regular medical check-ups Buy a gym or sports club membership
Your work environment	Buy a more ergonomic chair and desk Change your lightbulbs to warmer ones Install a fan or air conditioner in your work area Rent a larger workspace with more airflow and sunlight
People to support you	Hire more staff to join your team Contract with a freelance consultant Work with a virtual online secretarial service Upskill and train your staff
Your tools	Upgrade your laptop to a faster one with more hard disk space Change to faster internet broadband Subscribe to a data backup service Start using paid productivity apps, software solutions and other paid online services
Your processes and systems	Invest in automating some of your time-consuming and error-filled manual processes Move systems online and store data on the Cloud
Your learning	Go back to school by paying for a course at your local college, business school or online learning platform Invest in relevant books, training courses or a coach

Identify the benefits

If you're able to expense these purchases, your only challenge will be to make a good case to your boss to have them approve your expense claim. If you're paying out of your own pocket, you may be reluctant to part with your money, but think of the expense as an investment which will have a financial return, and try to visualize what this may be, such as time saved by automating manual processes.

BE OPEN ABOUT YOUR GOALS

Hold yourself accountable by telling others your goals and plans.

It will be easier to achieve your aims if you share details about them with other people. This was confirmed in 2016 research published by the American Psychological Association which analysed 138 studies and concluded that your chance of achieving your goals is increased when you publicly share and report them. The benefits of being open include:

- the sense of not being alone when you have someone who understands what you're trying to achieve
- the added motivation of having someone supporting and holding you accountable
- the possibility of discussing your goals and of receiving feedback and advice.

For this to work you shouldn't share with just anyone. Only choose people who'll be interested, helpful and supportive, and most importantly select those you admire and respect. This was the conclusion of a 2020 study from Ohio State University, published in *the Journal of Applied Psychology*, which found that you demonstrate the most commitment to achieving goals when you share them with someone you look up to (often a more senior person of higher status). You're more likely to persist because you wouldn't want to let such a person down.

Keep the circle small and avoid the mistake of telling everyone around you. There's little benefit to announcing your goals widely and you run the risk that some people may be negative, cynical, jealous, and even try to undermine and sabotage your success.

Chapter 97

Find an accountability buddy

Your accountability buddy should tick the following four boxes:

1 You know them well.
2 They are interested in your success.
3 You trust and respect them.
4 You look up to and admire them.

They might be a senior colleague in your company, a mentor you've worked with in the past, a retired former boss or even one of your peers. Approach them and ask if they'd be willing to act as a kind of mentor and coach, explaining that you'll share your goals and plans with them and ask that in return they'll support and encourage you, while holding you accountable.

When you've found someone willing to help you, agree to meet (in person or online) on a regular basis to:

• understand your aims and goals
• explore how they may have changed over time
• monitor and review your progress towards achieving them
• celebrate any successes
• brainstorm about obstacles and challenges you're facing
• challenge you when you may be slowing down or showing signs of giving up.

In addition to work-focused goals, you can do the same thing with your personal and life goals, sharing them with a trusted friend or family member.

BE HONEST WITH YOURSELF

Fool anyone you want, but never fool yourself.

There's no point in reading this book, and trying to implement what you've learned, if you're not honest with yourself. Sadly, too many people aren't, and they become their own worst enemy when it comes to trying to be productive. You're probably familiar with the following scenarios that all arise out of being in denial:

- acting convinced that a revised sales forecast is achievable when you've seen data that clearly proves otherwise
- assuring yourself that you'll attend a team meeting tomorrow, when you know that you'll be unable to be back in time from a client visit
- acting mean, cold and difficult with your team members, while being in total denial about your poor behaviour
- telling yourself that you enjoy your job, when the truth is the opposite and it's bringing you down
- creating a long and detailed to-do list, telling yourself that it'll be completed by the end of the month, when it's obvious to you that the list of tasks is far too long and impossible to complete in time
- telling yourself and others that a challenging task you're working on will be ready by the requested deadline, when you're behind schedule in completing it and you know you won't finish on time
- convincing yourself that you're very happy with a project's progress to date, when in truth you have so many misgivings about it.

These are common examples because people don't like to admit that things aren't perfect and deal with the consequences. Productive people know that there's never any value to be gained in fooling yourself or those around you.

Know yourself

Try to understand the reasons why you're ignoring what should be obvious to you. Think of recent situations where you acted in denial, and ask yourself why you were willing to fool yourself. Was it because you were afraid of being honest with yourself and facing the consequences, including upsetting other people, or were you just blindly optimistic, refusing to believe a disappointing outcome might occur? It is possible that you weren't in denial at all and instead you simply didn't analyse the situation properly or were unaware of the facts.

Commit to being honest with yourself

Starting today, be totally honest and realistic with yourself, particularly when facing important situations and decisions. As a minimum commit to no longer:

- pretending you can achieve more than you're able to and agreeing to impossible deadlines
- fooling yourself into thinking you understand something about which you actually have little or no idea
- supporting something that you don't agree with
- saying 'yes' to yourself when you know the correct response is 'no'.

BECOME A SUBJECT MATTER EXPERT

Be willing to gain expertise in any field you work in.

Are you the go-to person for what you do? Expertise is an important productivity asset. When you have deep knowledge of your job function, work domain and the technology and processes you use, you will work more quickly and efficiently. By becoming an authority in your domain or field you'll be able to optimize your work performance through a combination of:

- being able to complete job responsibilities and tasks more easily
- being more accurate and precise, and making fewer mistakes
- having insights to improve processes and ways of working
- having the wisdom to solve new problems and situations
- boosting your confidence to take on more difficult challenges
- being able to support, mentor and train your colleagues.

You'll also have a competitive edge over other people, which will make you more valued within the company you work for.

Chapter **99**

Gain expertise in your chosen domain

Use the following tips to gain expertise in your domain:

- Make learning your highest priority by following the tips shared in Chapter 72. As a minimum, read relevant journals and professional publications.
- Throw yourself into your work, seeking out new challenges and opportunities to gain domain skills and knowledge. Use the advice shared in Chapter 40 about deliberately practising your new skills.
- Find someone who's already a domain expert and ask them to be your mentor. Chapter 57 tells you how to find and work with one.
- Join and participate in relevant associations. For example, if you want to become an expert in accounting standards, you might become an active and accredited member of a global accountancy body.
- Consider returning, full-time or part-time, to academia to deepen your knowledge of the latest theories, models, research and thinking in your domain.
- Attend conferences, expos and other events that cover the domain you want to excel in. Always take the time to listen to and talk with exhibitors and fellow attendees.

Teach and give back

As your knowledge grows, share your expertise by podcasting, writing blogs, articles and papers. You can also make yourself available to speak at relevant events.

Be available to mentor and teach your colleagues. This might pull you away from more urgent and important tasks, but you can solve this time management challenge by making 'being a subject matter expert' part of your job description. That way part of your working day can be formally allocated to teaching, helping and supporting your colleagues.

REVIEW YOUR PROGRESS

You think you're productive, but are you sure?

In order to successfully implement the numerous tools and pieces of advice contained in this book, there are three important qualities to bear in mind:

- patience
- a willingness to step back and review
- an openness to share what you've learned.

Becoming productive doesn't happen overnight. It's a journey of trial and error, successes and setbacks. New work challenges will require new thinking and solutions. It's easy to feel frustrated when your first attempts at creating to-do lists or organizing your working day don't yield immediate benefits, or when your hopes of creating more productive team meetings and a cleaner and healthier workspace don't seem to have the impact you were looking for.

Be patient and give yourself time. If you're doing the right things, then over time your efforts to be more productive will yield visible results.

Productive people take time to review what's working well and what requires more of their attention by assessing how well they're solving their productivity challenges. This is just the start of your journey. You'll need to continually adjust things so that you're able to work really smart and productively.

Conduct a productivity audit

Give yourself a couple of months to implement your new ways of working, then pause to reflect on how well you're doing.

- Recall those productivity problems you wanted to work on. Perhaps you needed to push back and say 'no' to requests for your time, get a better night's sleep or make better use of productivity apps.
- Analyse your progress to date in achieving these goals. You might get some feedback from colleagues, asking them if they've observed any improvements in specific areas of your work.
- Evaluate how well you're currently using any of the tools and ideas that you've learned about in this book.
- Celebrate any successes while committing to work hard on those goals that still need your attention.
- Based on any feedback and your own observations, create a new action plan for improving your productivity-enhancing skills.

Become an authority on getting things done

Now that you've come to the end of this book's 100 chapters, don't keep it all to yourself. Try to build on the subject matter expert concept in Chapter 99 by committing to become an authority on productivity. By sharing your insights and advice, you'll be leaving a positive legacy by helping your colleagues (and family and friends) who're struggling with deadlines, prioritizing, and achieving their goals.

AND FINALLY

Always be open to new and unexpected productivity ideas – doing whatever it takes to help maintain and raise your performance levels.

I hope the advice, ideas and words of wisdom throughout this book inspire you to become more successful in all aspects of your work and life.

Be open to building on the 100 things in the book, to finding new and exciting ways of becoming more productive with any type of task you want to complete.

I would really like to keep in touch and to hear how my book has helped you and inspired you to success. Please connect with me on Facebook, Twitter, LinkedIn or Instagram. Email me at nigel@silkroadpartnership.com.

REFERENCES

Chapter 2

E.J. Masicampon and Roy F. Baumeister (2011) 'Consider it done? Plan making can eliminate the cognitive effects of unfulfilled goals', *Journal of Personality and Social Psychology*, 20 June, available at: http://users.wfu.edu/masicaej/MasicampoBaumeister2011JPSP.pdf

Shamarukh Chowdhury (2016) 'The construct validity of active procrastination: Is it procrastination or purposeful delay?', available at: https://curve.carleton.ca/system/files/etd/0b56283e-c2fa-43a4-bc29-34f6e4783c66/etd_pdf/7ea0cbef842a6734eb5210f11138443b/chowdhury-theconstructvalidityofactiveprocrastination.pdf

Chapter 3

Sun reporter (2017) 'Make it snappy: Average Brit has an attention span of just 14 minutes, study finds', *The Sun*, 28 December, available at: https://www.thesun.co.uk/news/5222877/average-brit-has-an-attention-span-of-just-14-minutes-study-finds/

Emma Elsworthy (2017) 'Average British attention span is 14 minutes, research finds', *Independent*, 28 December, available at: https://www.independent.co.uk/news/uk/home-news/attention-span-average-british-person-tuned-concentration-mobile-phone-a8131156.htmlPomodorotechnique:https://en.wikipedia.org/wiki/Pomodoro_Technique

Chapter 4

Paul Alhola and Päivi Polo-Kantola (2007) 'Sleep deprivation: Impact on cognitive performance', Dove Medical Press, available at: https://www.ncbi.nlm.nih.gov/pmc/articles/PMC2656292/

Julian Lim and David F. Dinges (2008) 'Sleep deprivation and vigilant attention', available at: https://pubmed.ncbi.nlm.nih.gov/18591490/

Anna Puig-Ribera et al. (2017) 'Impact of a workplace "sit less, move more" program on efficiency-related outcomes of office employees', available at: https://pubmed.ncbi.nlm.nih.gov/28511642/

Jørgen Dejgård Jensen (2011) 'Can worksite nutritional interventions improve productivity and firm profitability? A literature review', *Perspectives in Public Health*, SAGE Journals, available at: https://journals.sagepub.com/doi/10.1177/1757913911408263

Tamlin S. Connor et al. (2015) 'On carrots and curiosity: Eating fruit and vegetables is associated with greater flourishing in daily life', *British Journal of Health Psychology*, available at: https://pubmed.ncbi.nlm.nih.gov/25080035/

Chapter 7

The Myers-Briggs Company (2019) 'Type and the always-on culture', available at: https://www.themyersbriggs.com/-/media/Myers-Briggs/Files/Resources-Hub-Files/Research/Type_and_the_always_on_culture.pdf

Chapter 8

McKinsey Global Institute (2012) 'The social economy: Unlocking value and productivity through social technologies', available at: https://www.mckinsey.com/industries/technology-media-and-telecommunications/our-insights/the-social-economy

Kronos (2018) 'Time well spent? New survey explores the case for a 4-day work week', available at: https://www.kronos.com/blogs/working-smarter-cafe/time-well-spent-new-survey-explores-case-4-day-work-week

Vouchercloud, 'How many productive hours in a work day? Just 2 hours, 23 minutes...', available at: https://www.vouchercloud.com/resources/office-worker-productivity

Chapter 9

Samuel E. Jones et al. (2019) 'Genome-wide association analyses of chronotype in 697,828 individuals provides insights into circadian rhythms', *Nature*

Communications 10(343), available at: https://www.nature.com/articles/s41467-018-08259-7?utm_medium=affiliate&utm_source=commission_junction&utm_campaign=3_nsn6445_deeplink_PID100090071&utm_content=deeplink

Martha Hotz Vitaterna, Joseph S. Takahashi and Fred Turek (2019) 'Overview of circadian rhythms', National Institute on Alcohol Abuse and Alcoholism, available at: https://pubs.niaaa.nih.gov/publications/arh25-2/85-93.htm

Chapter 11

McKinsey & Company (2021) 'Defining the skills citizens will need in the future world of work', available at: https://www.mckinsey.com/industries/public-and-social-sector/our-insights/defining-the-skills-citizens-will-need-in-the-future-world-of-work

Chapter 12

Commencement address delivered by Steve Jobs, CEO of Apple Computer and of Pixar Animation Studios (2005), available at: https://news.stanford.edu/2005/06/14/jobs-061505/

Flow: https://en.wikipedia.org/wiki/Flow_(psychology)

Patricia Chen, Phoebe C. Ellsworth and Norbert Schwarz (2015) 'Finding a fit or developing it: Implicit theories about achieving passion for work', *Personality and Social Psychology Bulletin*, available at: https://journals.sagepub.com/doi/abs/10.1177/0146167215596988

Chapter 13

Dana Harari et al. (2018) 'Is perfect good? A meta-analysis of perfectionism in the workplace', *Journal of Applied Psychology* 103(10), available at: https://psycnet.apa.org/record/2018-27801-001

Murray W. Enns, Brian Cox and Ian Clara (2002) 'Adaptive and maladaptive perfectionism: Developmental origins and association with depression proneness', *Personality and Individual Differences* 33(6), available at: https://www.sciencedirect.com/science/article/abs/pii/S0191886901002021

Chapter 14

Katrin B. Klingsieck (2013) 'When good things don't come to those who wait', *Open Science in Psychology* 18(1), available at: https://econtent.hogrefe.com/doi/full/10.1027/1016-9040/a000138

Piers Steel (2007) 'The nature of procrastination', American Psychological Association, University of Calgary, available at: https://prism.ucalgary.ca/bitstream/handle/1880/47914/Steel_PsychBulletin_2007_Postprint.pdf;jsessionid=2BEED5339584820A7891AAB9479A05AA?sequence=1

Zeigarnik effect: https://en.wikipedia.org/wiki/Zeigarnik_effect

Chapter 16

Melissa Webster (2012) 'Bridging the information worker productivity gap: New challenges and opportunities for IT', White Paper, IDC Analyze the Future, available at: https://warekennis.nl/wp-content/uploads/2013/11/bridging-the-information-worker-productivity-gap.pdf

Elizabeth Sander, Arran Caza and Peter J. Jordan (2019) 'Psychological perceptions matter: Developing the reactions to the physical work environment scale', *Building and Environment* 148, available at: https://www.sciencedirect.com/science/article/abs/pii/S0360132318307157

Catherine A. Roster and Joseph R. Ferran (2019) 'Does work stress lead to office clutter, and how? Mediating influences of emotional exhaustion and indecision', *Environment and Behavior*, available at: https://journals.sagepub.com/doi/abs/10.1177/0013916518823041?casa_token=yQLToPTHinAAAAAA%3AMgAqBDvc_MIH7UAWMZqtKLy1ZP7Rtr_SF0c_OnN20oPQuo89W5U8uc PHg6gjwShwy430Pj2tytLc&

Terrence G. Horgan, Noelle K. Herzog and Sarah M. Dyszlewski (2019) 'Does your messy office make your mind look cluttered? Office appearance and perceivers' judgments about the owner's personality', *Personality and Individual Differences*, 138, available at: https://www.sciencedirect.com/science/article/abs/pii/S019188691830549X

Kathleen D. Vohs, Joseph P. Redden and Ryan Rahinel (2013) 'Physical order produces healthy choices, generosity, and conventionality, whereas disorder produces creativity', *Psychological Science*, available at: https://journals.sagepub.com/doi/abs/10.1177/0956797613480186

Chapter 18

Robert C. Pozen and Keven Downey (2019) 'What makes some people more productive than others', *Harvard Business Review*, 28 March, available at: https://hbr.org/2019/03/what-makes-some-people-more-productive-than-others

Chapter 19

Tom Rowlands (2020) 'The average worker has 651 unread emails in their inbox', *Pure Property Finance*, available at: https://www.purepropertyfinance.co.uk/news/the-average-worker-has-651-unread-emails-in-their-inbox/

André Spicer (2019) 'How many work emails is too many?', *The Guardian*, 8 April, available at: https://www.theguardian.com/technology/shortcuts/2019/apr/08/how-many-work-emails-is-too-many

Kristin Naragon (2018) 'We still love email, but we're spreading the love with other channels', Adobe Experience Cloud Blog, available at: https://blog.adobe.com/en/publish/2018/08/21/love-email-but-spreading-the-love-other-channels.html#gs.8gcle

McKinsey Global Institute (2012) 'The social economy: Unlocking value and productivity through social technologies', 1 July, available at: https://www.mckinsey.com/industries/technology-media-and-telecommunications/our-insights/the-social-economy#

UCI News (2012) 'Jettisoning work email reduces stress', 3 May, available at: https://news.uci.edu/2012/05/03/jettisoning-work-email-reduces-stress/

Chapter 20

Harvard Business School (2019) 'Task selection and workload: A focus on completing easy tasks hurts performance', available at: https://papers.ssrn.com/sol3/papers.cfm?abstract_id=2992588

Chapter 21

Science Daily (2016) 'Dopamine: Far more than just the "happy hormone"', available at: https://www.sciencedaily.com/releases/2016/08/160831085320.htm

Parkinson's Law, https://en.wikipedia.org/wiki/Parkinson%27s_law

Chapter 22

Korn Ferry (2019) 'Working or wasting time?', available at: https://www.kornferry.com/about-us//press/working-or-wasting-time

Michael Mankins, Chris Brahm and Greg Caimi (2014) 'Your scarcest resource', *Harvard Business Review*, May, available at: https://hbr.org/2014/05/your-scarcest-resource

Steven G. Rogelberg (2020) 'Remote meetings', *MIT Sloan Management Review*, 21 May, available at: https://sloanreview.mit.edu/article/the-surprising-science-behind-successful-remote-meetings/

Chapter 23

Susan Sorenson (nd) 'How employees' strengths make your company stronger', Gallup, available at: https://www.gallup.com/workplace/231605/employees-strengths-company-stronger.aspx

Chapter 25

Stacy E. Walker (2006) 'Journal writing as a teaching technique to promote reflection', *Journal of Athletic Training* 41(2), available at: https://www.ncbi.nlm.nih.gov/pmc/articles/PMC1472640/

Chapter 26

Ayelet Fishbach and Minjung Koo (2008) 'Dynamics of self-regulation: How (un)accomplished goal actions affect motivation', *Journal of Personality and Social Psychology* 94(2), available at: https://psycnet.apa.org/record/2008-00466-001

Chapter 27

American Psychological Association (2001) 'Multitasking undermines our efficiency, study suggests', available at: https://www.apa.org/monitor/oct01/multitask

Adam Gorlick (2009) 'Media multitaskers pay mental price, Stanford study shows', Stanford Report, 24 August, available at: https://news.stanford.edu/news/2009/august24/multitask-research-study-082409.html

University of Sussex (2014) 'Brain scans reveal "gray matter" differences in media multitaskers', available at: https://www.eurekalert.org/news-releases/467495

Garth Sundem (2012) 'This is your brain on multitasking', *Psychology Today*, 24 February, available at: https://www.psychologytoday.com/us/blog/brain-trust/201202/is-your-brain-multitasking

Chapter 28

Susan Weinschenk (2012) 'Why we're all addicted to texts, Twitter and Google', *Psychology Today*, 11 September, available at: https://www.psychologytoday.com/gb/blog/brain-wise/201209/why-were-all-addicted-texts-twitter-and-google

Screen Education (2020) 'Screen Education's "Distraction & workplace safety" survey finds US employees distracted 2.5 hours each workday by digital content unrelated to their jobs', available at: https://www.prnewswire.com/news-releases/screen-educations-smartphone-distraction--workplace-safety-survey-finds-us-employees-distracted-2-5-hours-each-workday-by-digital-content-unrelated-to-their-jobs-301120969.html

Florida State University (2015) 'Cell phone alerts may be driving you to distraction', available at: https://www.fsu.edu/indexTOFStory.html?lead.distraction

UT News (2017) 'The mere presence of your smartphone reduces brain power, study shows', available at: https://news.utexas.edu/2017/06/26/the-mere-presence-of-your-smartphone-reduces-brain-power/

Chapter 29

Nelson Cowan (2010) 'The magical mystery four: How is working memory capacity limited and why?', *Current Directions in Psychological Science* 19(1), available at: https://www.ncbi.nlm.nih.gov/pmc/articles/PMC2864034/

Gantt chart: https://en.wikipedia.org/wiki/Gantt_chart

Chapter 30

Richard W. Goggins, Peregrin Spielholz and Greg Nothstein (2008) 'Estimating the effectiveness of ergonomics interventions through case studies: Implications for predictive cost-benefit analysis', *Journal of Safety Research* 39(3), available at: https://pubmed.ncbi.nlm.nih.gov/18571576/

Chapter 31

Ayelet Gnezy and Nicholas Epley (2014) 'Worth keeping but not exceeding: Asymmetric consequences of breaking versus exceeding promises', *Social Psychological and Personality Science*, 8 May, available at: https://journals.sagepub.com/doi/abs/10.1177/1948550614533134

Chapter 32

Harvard Business School (2002) 'Great performances – the five keys to successful teams', available at: https://hbswk.hbs.edu/archive/leading-teams-setting-the-stage-for-great-performances-the-five-keys-to-successful-teams

Caroline Aubé, Vincent Rousseau and Sébastien Tremblay (2011) 'Team size and quality of group experience: The more the merrier?', *Group Dynamics: Theory, Research, and Practice* 15(4), available at: https://www.researchgate.net/publication/232519143_Team_Size_and_Quality_of_Group_Experience_The_More_the_Merrier

Chapter 33

SMART criteria: https://en.wikipedia.org/wiki/SMART_criteria

Chapter 34

John Whitmore (racing driver): https://en.wikipedia.org/wiki/John_Whitmore_(racing_driver)

Chapter 36

Pareto principle: https://en.wikipedia.org/wiki/Pareto_principle

Chapter 37

Udemy (2018) 'Udemy In Depth: 2018 Workplace Distraction Report', available at: https://research.udemy.com/research_report/udemy-depth-2018-workplace-distraction-report/

Atsunori Ariga and Alejandro Lleras (2011) 'Brief and rare mental "breaks" keep you focused: Deactivation and reactivation of task goals preempt vigilance decrements', *Cognition* 118(3), available at: https://pubmed.ncbi.nlm.nih.gov/21211793/

Chapter 38

Accenture (2015) 'Accenture research finds listening more difficult in today's digital workplace', available at: https://newsroom.accenture.com/industries/global-media-industry-analyst-relations/accenture-research-finds-listening-more-difficult-in-todays-digital-workplace.htm

Norris Wise (2018) 'Listening and its impact on productivity in the workplace', *Journal of Psychology & Psychotherapy*, 19 September, available at: https://www.longdom.org/proceedings/listening-and-its-impact-on-productivity-in-the-workplace-12954.html

Chapter 39

Vincent R. Brown and Paul B. Pauls (2002) 'Making group brainstorming more effective: Recommendations from an associative memory perspective', *Current Directions in Psychological Science*, available at: https://journals.sagepub.com/doi/10.1111/1467-8721.00202

Chapter 40

David Hambrick (2014) 'Accounting for expert performance: The devil is in the details', *Intelligence*, available at: https://www.sciencedirect.com/science/article/abs/pii/S0160289614000087

Chapter 42

Corinna Peifer et al. (2020) 'Well done! Effects of positive feedback on perceived self-efficacy, flow and performance in a mental arithmetic task', *Frontiers in Psychology*, 10 June, available at: https://www.frontiersin.org/articles/10.3389/fpsyg.2020.01008/full

Jack Zenger and Joseph Folkman (2013) 'Overcoming feedback phobia: Take the first step', *Harvard Business Review*, 16 December, available at: https://hbr.org/2013/12/overcoming-feedback-phobia-take-the-first-step

Chapter 44

McKenzie Hyde (nd) 'Making the most of the morning', Amersleep, available at: https://amerisleep.com/blog/making-the-most-of-the-morning/

Adriane M. Soehner, Kathy S. Kennedy and Timothy H. Monk (2011) 'Circadian preference and sleep-wake regularity: Associations with self-report sleep parameters in daytime-working adults', *Chronobiology International* 28(9), available at: https://pubmed.ncbi.nlm.nih.gov/22080786/

Jacob A. Nota and Meredith E. Coles (2014) 'Duration and timing of sleep are associated with repetitive negative thinking', *Cognitive Therapy and Research* 39, available at: https://link.springer.com/article/10.1007/s10608-014-9651-7?wt_mc=Affiliate.CommissionJunction.3.EPR1089.DeepLink&utm_medium=affiliate&utm_source=commission_junction&utm_campaign=3_nsn6445_deeplink&utm_content=deeplink

Hal Elrod (2016), The Miracle Morning: https://www.hachette.co.uk/titles/hal-elrod/the-miracle-morning/9781473632165/

Chapter 46

Robert Half (2018) 'Meeting of the minds: Workers and executives dread wasted time, disengagement', Robert Half news releases, available at: https://rh-us.mediaroom.com/2018-07-31-Meeting-Of-The-Minds-Workers-And-Executives-Dread-Wasted-Time-Disengagement

Doodle (2019), 'The state of meetings 2019', available at: https://doodle.com/en/resources/research-and-reports-/the-state-of-meetings-2019/

Chapter 47

Robert Half (2018) 'Time spent (and wasted) in meetings', The Robert Half Blog, available at: https://www.roberthalf.com/blog/management-tips/time-spent-and-wasted-in-meetings

Science Daily (2011) 'Brief diversions vastly improve focus, researchers find', University of Illinois at Urbana-Champaign, available at: https://www.sciencedaily.com/releases/2011/02/110208131529.htm

Chapter 48

Gallup (2018) 'Employee burnout, part 1: The 5 main causes', 12 July, available at: https://www.gallup.com/workplace/237059/employee-burnout-part-main-causes.aspx

Chapter 49

Getting Things Done: https://en.wikipedia.org/wiki/Getting_Things_Done

Chapter 50

Gillian Weston et al. (2019) 'Long work hours, weekend working and depressive symptoms in men and women: Findings from a UK population-based study', *Journal of Epidemiology and Community Health* 73(5), available at: https://www.ncbi.nlm.nih.gov/pmc/articles/PMC6581113/

Andrew M. Bryce (2019) 'Weekend working in 21st century Britain: Does it matter for wellbeing?', Sheffield Economic Research Series, University of Sheffield, available at: https://www.sheffield.ac.uk/media/3802/download

Chapter 51

Asana (nd) 'Anatomy of Work Index: How people spend their time at work', available at: https://resources.asana.com/rs/784-XZD-582/images/Anatomy-of-Work-Index.pdf

Chapter 54

US Department of Energy Office of Scientific and Technical Information (2003) 'Cost benefit analysis of the night-time ventilative cooling in office building', available at: https://www.osti.gov/servlets/purl/813396

Interface Study (2019) 'Interface study reveals impact of noise on workplace productivity', available at: https://iands.design/articles/32955/interface-study-reveals-impact-noise-workplace-productivity

Joseph G. Allen (2017) 'Research: Stale office air is making you less productive', *Harvard Business Review*, 21 March, available at: https://hbr.org/2017/03/research-stale-office-air-is-making-you-less-productive

Jo Silvester and Efrosyni Konstantinou (nd) 'Lighting, well-being and performance at work', Centre for Performance at Work, available at: https://www.bayes.city.ac.uk/__data/assets/pdf_file/0004/363217/lighting-work-performance-cass.pdf

Chapter 56

Christie Smith (2021) 'Accenture Future of Work Study 2021', Accenture, available at: https://www.accenture.com/us-en/insights/consulting/future-work?c=acn_glb_talentandorganimediarelations_12163686&tn=mrl_0521

The Adecco Group (nd) 'Resetting normal: Defining the new era of work 2021', available at: https://www.adeccogroup.com/future-of-work/latest-research/resetting-normal-2021/#download-the-global-report

Chapter 57

EMCC Global (nd) 'Definition of mentoring', available at: https://www.emccglobal.org/leadership-development/leadership-development-mentoring/

Henry Blodget (2003) 'Warren Buffett and Bill Gates explain how to make $100 billion...', *Insider*, 15 November, available at: https://www.businessinsider.com/henry-blodget-warren-buffett-and-bill-gates-on-cnbc-2009-11?op=1&r=US&IR=T#why-did-you-buy-burlington-northern-1

Alison Coleman (2016) 'Why mentors can be the making of entrepreneurs like Branson', *Forbes*, 10 April, available at: https://www.forbes.com/sites/alisoncoleman/2016/04/10/why-mentors-can-be-the-making-of-entrepreneurs-like-branson/?sh=5bdfd3c51778

Chapter 59

Forgetting curve: https://en.wikipedia.org/wiki/Forgetting_curve

Guido Hertel (nd) 'Why forgetting at work can be a good thing', University of Münster, available at: https://www.uni-muenster.de/news/view.php?cmdid=10075&lang=en

Chapter 61

British Heart Foundation (nd) 'Are you sitting too much?', available at: https://www.bhf.org.uk/informationsupport/heart-matters-magazine/activity/sitting-down

Gregory Garrett et al. (2016) 'Call center productivity over 6 months following a standing desk intervention', *IIE Transactions on Occupational Ergonomics and Human Factors*, available at: https://www.tandfonline.com/doi/abs/10.1080/21577323.2016.1183534

Charlotte Edwardson et al. (2018) 'Effectiveness of the Stand More AT (SMArT) Work intervention: Cluster randomised controlled trial', *British Medical Journal* 363, available at: https://www.bmj.com/content/363/bmj.k3870

Seth A. Creasy et al. (2016) 'Energy expenditure during acute periods of sitting, standing, and walking', *Journal of Physical Activity and Health* 13(6), available at: https://pubmed.ncbi.nlm.nih.gov/26693809/

Andrew P. Knight and Markus Baer (2014) 'Get up, stand up: The effects of a non-sedentary workspace on information elaboration and group performance', *Social Psychological and Personality Science*, 12 June, available at: https://journals.sagepub.com/doi/abs/10.1177/1948550614538463

Chapter 62

Will Dahlgreen (2015) 'More than a third of British workers say their job is making no meaningful contribution to the world – but most of them aren't looking for another one', 12 August, YouGov, available at: https://yougov.co.uk/topics/lifestyle/articles-reports/2015/08/12/british-jobs-meaningless

Rutger Bregman (2017) 'A growing number of people think their job is useless. Time to rethink the meaning of work', World Economic Forum, available at: https://www.weforum.org/agenda/2017/04/why-its-time-to-rethink-the-meaning-of-work/

Fyodor Dostoevsky: https://www.goodreads.com/quotes/6715871-if-one-wanted-to-crush-and-destroy-a-man-entirely

Chapter 63

John Pencavel (2014) 'The productivity of working hours', Discussion Paper, IZA, available at: https://ftp.iza.org/dp8129.pdf

Erin Reid (2015) 'Why some men pretend to work 80-hour weeks', *Harvard Business Review*, 28 April, available at: https://hbr.org/2015/04/why-some-men-pretend-to-work-80-hour-weeks

Ruo Shangguan (2021) 'Enhancing team productivity through shorter working hours: Evidence from the Great Recession', Research Institute of Economy, Trade and Industry, Research Project, available at: https://www.rieti.go.jp/en/publications/summary/21050007.html

Chapter 65

Ben Ready (2017) 'Communication skills most valued by employers', MBA news, available at: https://www.mbanews.com.au/communication-skills-valued-employers/

Fran Molloy (2018) 'Top 10 employability skills', Careers with STEM, available at: https://careerswithstem.com.au/employability-skills/

Lou Solomon (2016) 'Two-thirds of managers are uncomfortable communicating with employees', *Harvard Business Review*, 9 March, available at: https://hbr.org/2016/03/two-thirds-of-managers-are-uncomfortable-communicating-with-employees?zd_source=hrt&zd_campaign=3731&zd_term=vartikakashyap

Chapter 66

Teresa M. Amabile and Steven J. Kramer (2011) 'The power of small wins', *Harvard Business Review*, May, available at: https://hbr.org/2011/05/the-power-of-small-wins

Chapter 67

Cal Newport: https://en.wikipedia.org/wiki/Cal_Newport

Chapter 68

Five stages of grief: https://en.wikipedia.org/wiki/Five_stages_of_grief

Nigel Cumberland (2021), 100 Things Successful People Do: https://www.hachette.co.uk/titles/nigel-cumberland/100-things-successful-people-do/9781529395266/

Chapter 71

Saeedeh Ahmadi (2020) 'Stretch goals can have negative outcomes', RSM, available at: https://discovery.rsm.nl/articles/419-stretch-goals-can-have-negative-outcomes/

Michael Shayne Gary et al. (2017) 'Performance', available at: https://pubsonline.informs.org/doi/10.1287/orsc.2017.1131

Chapter 72

Marguerite Ward (2016) 'Warren Buffett's reading routine could make you smarter, science suggests', Make It, 16 November, available at: https://www.cnbc.com/2016/11/16/warren-buffetts-reading-routine-could-make-you-smarter-suggests-science.html

Marie Speed (2015) 'Tony Robbins on how to achieve the extraordinary', *Success*, 4 January, available at: https://www.success.com/tony-robbins-on-how-to-achieve-the-extraordinary/

Melissa Webster (2012) 'Bridging the information worker productivity gap: New challenges and opportunities for IT', IDC Analyze the Future, September, available at: https://warekennis.nl/wp-content/uploads/2013/11/bridging-the-information-worker-productivity-gap.pdf

Chapter 75

Sudip Bhattacharya, Sheikh Saleem and Amarjeet Singh (2020) 'Digital eye strain in the era of COVID-19 pandemic', *Indian Journal of Ophthalmology* 68(8), available at: https://journals.lww.com/ijo/fulltext/2020/68080/digital_eye_strain_in_the_era_of_covid_19.69.aspx

Anne-Marie Chang et al. (2014) 'Evening use of light-emitting eReaders negatively affects sleep, circadian timing and next-morning alertness', Proceedings of the National Academy of Sciences, available at: https://www.pnas.org/content/pnas/112/4/1232.full.pdf

Ariel Shensa et al. (2018) 'Social media use and depression and anxiety symptoms: A cluster analysis', *American Journal of Health Behavior*, 42(2), available at: https://www.pnas.org/content/pnas/112/4/1232.full.pdf

Chapter 76

Joshua S. Rubinstein, David E. Meyer and Jeffrey Evans (2001) 'Executive control of cognitive processes in task switching', *Journal of Experimental Psychology: Human Perception and Performance* 27(4), available at: https://psycnet.apa.org/record/2001-07721-001

Chapter 78

Lien B. Pham and Shelley E. Taylor (1999) 'From thought to action: Effects of process- versus outcome-based mental simulations on performance', *Personality and Social Psychology Bulletin* 25(2), available at: https://psycnet.apa.org/record/1999-00580-010

Chapter 79

Mel Robbins: https://en.wikipedia.org/wiki/Mel_Robbins

Chapter 80

University of Sheffield (2016) 'Does monitoring goal progress promote goal attainment? A meta-analysis of the experimental evidence', *Psychological Bulletin* 142(2), available at: https://www.apa.org/pubs/journals/releases/bul-bul0000025.pdf

Chapter 82

Cecil Schou Andreassen et al. (2014) 'The prevalence of workaholism: A survey study in a nationally representative sample of Norwegian employees', PLOS ONE, 13 August, available at: https://journals.plos.org/plosone/article?id=10.1371/journal.pone.0102446

Tyler Small (2019) 'Almost half of Americans consider themselves "workaholics"', *New York Post*, 1 February, available at: https://nypost.com/2019/02/01/almost-half-of-americans-consider-themselves-workaholics/

Cecile Schou Andreassen et al. (2012) 'Development of a work addiction scale', *Scandinavian Journal of Psychology* 53(3), available at: https://www.research-gate.net/publication/223971523_Development_of_a_work_addiction_scale

Rachel Sharp (2016) 'Work addiction risk test', *Occupational Medicine* 56(4), available at: https://academic.oup.com/occmed/article/66/4/341/1752189

Chapter 84

Carl Binder (nd) 'The Six Boxes TM: A descendent of Gilbert's Behavior Engineering Model', available at: https://www.sixboxes.com/_customelements/uploadedResources/SixBoxes.pdf

Chapter 85

Erik Brynjolfsson, Tom Mitchell and Daniel Rock (2018) 'What can machines learn, and what does it mean for occupations and the economy?', *AEA Papers and Proceedings* 108, American Economic Association, available at: https://www.aeaweb.org/articles?id=10.1257/pandp.20181019

Tom Relihan (2018) 'Machine learning will redesign, not replace, work', *MIT Management*, 26 June, available at: https://mitsloan.mit.edu/ideas-made-to-matter/machine-learning-will-redesign-not-replace-work

AI predictions 2021, PwC, available at: https://www.pwc.com/us/en/tech-effect/ai-analytics/ai-predictions.html

Chapter 86

Arnold B. Bakker et al. (2020) 'Job crafting and playful work design: Links with performance during busy and quiet days', *Journal of Vocational Behavior* 122, available at: https://www.researchgate.net/publication/343811272_Job_crafting_and_playful_work_design_Links_with_performance_during_busy_and_quiet_days

Claire Aslinn Petelczyc, Alessandra Capezio and Lu Want (2017) 'Play at work: An integrative review and agenda for future research', *Journal of Management*, 26 September, available at: https://journals.sagepub.com/doi/abs/10.1177/0149206317731519

Daniel Scroy (2015) 'Happiness and productivity: Understanding the happy-productive worker', Social Market Foundation, available at: https://www.ciphr.com/wp-content/uploads/2016/11/Social-Market-Foundation-Publication-Briefing-CAGE-4-Are-happy-workers-more-productive-281015.pdf

Chapter 90

Science Daily (2008) 'Working alone may be the key to better productivity, new research suggests', University of Calgary, available at: https://www.sciencedaily.com/releases/2008/02/080220110323.htm

Julian Birkinshaw, Jordan Cohen and Pawel Stach (2020) 'Research: Knowledge workers are more productive from home', *Harvard Business Review*, 31 August, available at: https://hbr.org/2020/08/research-knowledge-workers-are-more-productive-from-home

Imke Kirste et al. (2013) 'Is silence golden? Effects of auditory stimuli and their absence on adult hippocampal neurogenesis', *Brain Structure and Function* 220, available at: https://link.springer.com/article/10.1007%2 Fs00429-013-0679-3

Jenni Radun et al. (2021) 'Speech is special: The stress effects of speech, noise, and silence during tasks requiring concentration', *Indoor Air* 31(1), available at: https://pubmed.ncbi.nlm.nih.gov/32805749/

Chapter 92

BusinessNewsWales (2019) 'Barclays finds the SME lightbulb moment most common at 2.33am', available at: https://businessnewswales.com/barclays-finds-the-sme-lightbulb-moment-most-common-at-2-33am/

Chapter 93

David McClelland: https://en.wikipedia.org/wiki/David_McClelland

Catherine T. Shea, Erin K. Davisson and Grainne M. Fitzsimons (2013) 'Riding other people's coattails: Individuals with low self-control value self-control in other people', *Psychological Science*, 4 April, available at: https://journals.sagepub.com/doi/abs/10.1177/0956797612464890?journalCode=pssa

Chapter 94

Priyanka B. Carr and Gregory M. Walton (2014) 'Cues of working together fuel intrinsic motivation', *Journal of Experimental Social Psychology* 53, available at: https://www.sciencedirect.com/science/article/abs/pii/S0022103114000420?via%3Dihub

Chapter 95

Becky Snowden (nd) 'A third of adults have fallen out with someone after misreading text messages, according to research', available at: https://www.thefreelibrary.com/Brits+falling+out+after+misreading+text+messages+and+spend+hours...-a0676421592

M. Mahdi Roghanizad and Vanessa K. Bohns (2017) 'Ask in person: You're less persuasive than you think over email', *Journal of Experimental Social Psychology* 69, available at: https://www.sciencedirect.com/science/article/abs/pii/S002210311630292X

Science Daily (2020) 'Phone calls create stronger bonds than text-based communications', University of Texas at Austin, 11 September, available at: https://www.sciencedaily.com/releases/2020/09/200911141713.htm

Albert Mehrabian: https://www.psych.ucla.edu/faculty-page/mehrab/

Chapter 97

American Psychological Association (2016) 'Does monitoring goal progress promote goal attainment? A meta-analysis of the experimental evidence', *Psychological Bulletin* 142(2), available at: https://www.apa.org/pubs/journals/releases/bul-bul0000025.pdf

Howard J. Klein et al. (2020) 'When goals are known: The effects of audience relative status on goal commitment and performance', *Journal of Applied Psychology* 105(4), available at: https://psycnet.apa.org/record/2019-45131-001